It was the ⸻ ⸻ sharing.

One mid-fifties man, who was seated in the medically exempt row for a back problem, spoke about what had gone on for him upon arising in the morning.

"I got up and did my exercises as I do each morning. Then I joined my wife for breakfast. I sat there looking at her and this great sadness came over me. Suddenly I realized why my back hurt so much all these years. It was my guarantee that Emily would pay attention to me upon command. For the twenty-five years we have been married, I was never able to tell her how much I need her. And I didn't tell her this morning. But I hope before the training is over that I can."

That husband is only one of the thousands of people who are learning—through est— to become lifetime winners, despite the problems and failures of the years gone by.

est: 4 DAYS TO MAKE YOUR LIFE WORK
is an original POCKET BOOK edition.

est:

4 Days to Make Your Life Work

by

William Greene

PUBLISHED BY POCKET BOOKS NEW YORK

It is important that the reader understand that all of the information in this book is based upon the experience of the author and numerous conversations with other est graduates and volunteers. It does not reflect the official est opinion; and one can be sure there is an official est opinion on everything in this book. Policy prohibits staff members from speaking directly to the media. All such requests are forwarded to the est Public Information Office. The information is all accurate and based on the author's research, but is in no way designed to reflect the feelings, policies, or beliefs of either Werner Erhard or est.

est: 4 DAYS TO MAKE YOUR LIFE WORK

POCKET BOOK edition published May, 1976

This original POCKET BOOK edition is printed from brand-new plates made from newly set, clear, easy-to-read type.
POCKET BOOK editions are published by
POCKET BOOKS,
a division of Simon & Schuster, Inc.,
A GULF+WESTERN COMPANY
630 Fifth Avenue,
New York, N.Y. 10020.
Trademarks registered in the United States and other countries.

ISBN: 0-671-80600-9.

to
Caroline

CONTENTS

CHAPTER I

What Is This Thing Called est?

What is the latest pop-psychological movement that is taking the country by storm? What topic is being discussed intimately at all the "with it" cocktail parties? It's America's fastest-growing phenomenon. It's Erhard Seminars Training—commonly known as est. Over 70,000 people from all walks of life have already graduated from est. Doctors, psychologists, housewives, lawyers, business executives, and society's dropouts all have est in common. They have loved it and hated it, but practically all of them agree on one thing: they have profited from it emotionally.

What Is This Thing Called est?

Always written in the lower case, it is an acronym for Erhard Seminars Training. Latin for "it is." "est is." Based in San Francisco, it is an organization staffed primarily by volunteers.

If est is examined on a superficial basis, it would be

easy to conclude that an est training program is comprised of a number of people who go to a hotel for two consecutive weekends and get:

1. No food.
2. Little opportunity to go to the bathroom.
3. Nothing to sit on but hard, straight-backed chairs for endless hours.
4. Yelled and screamed at during the training period.

On a personal level, est represents an opportunity to provide an individual with what might be the greatest sixty hours of his life.

Basically, the training is put together in three parts:

1. The trainer delivers a lecture and provides the trainee with information. (This is what est calls "the Data.")
2. The trainees talk about their own experiences or beliefs, related and nonrelated to the lecture and information. (This is what est calls "the Sharing.")
3. The trainees go through processes where they get in touch with what's coming up in their consciousness. (This is what est calls "the Processes.")

These three parts may run consecutively during any given day of the training or they may be used individually. For example, one day the trainees may do several different "processes" in a row, such as one to relax them and one to work out a specific emotion. Or the trainer may deliver a lecture, then provide time for sharing, and then run everyone through a single process.

est is an experience and, therefore, it is a very personalized kind of training. Each person reacts individually to it. The average training starts off with about 250 people. During the course of the training, somewhere between five and ten people will drop out at the est designated withdrawal periods. These people will receive a full refund. Those people who choose to leave at any other time may do so, but they will lose their $250 payment. (Most often, this occurs at a break, but occasionally they will storm out while the training is in progress. At that point, the trainer decides whether or not to physically let the person go, as the room is locked.)

What Is "Getting It"?

The basic goal of the est training is to "Get It." "Getting It" can be many things (including nothing). But, basically, it is accepting the fact that people are nothing more than machines, and that everything they have done in life to date has been based on faulty belief systems and misconceptions about themselves. Once a person can accept that he or she is a machine, the individual is capable of looking at this "machine" and making it disappear. By doing this, in theory, the individual is then experiencing life and being in the here and now.

"Getting It" has as many interpretations as there are trainees in any given program. For example, one of the things most trainees "Get" is that they would rather be right than alive. In order to be right, the individual sets it up so that someone else is wrong. This reinforces the rightness. That's the good news. The bad news is that the individual loses his sense of aliveness as a result. This directly interferes with his ability to fully communicate his real feelings and emotions to other people.

Although the est training is a highly personalized experience, and it is often stated that it cannot be clearly explained as a result, there are some basic tenets of the est philosophy that are included in "Getting It." They are:

1. Appropriate behavior. According to Werner Erhard, the founder of est, everyone is perfect the way he or she is. It's okay to be okay, and it's okay not to be okay. Simply interpreted, it would seem okay to kill people or physically harm them. That is not in the realm of appropriate behavior. It is not okay to inflict pain on other people.

2. Breaking agreements. Life doesn't work for most people because they are constantly breaking agreements. They are habitually late, or compromising their principles, or changing situations to suit their whims. People have got to make agreements with others and keep them.

3. Telling lies. Individuals are not truthful with others and themselves. Truth is the beginning of aliveness. In order to reach the level of aliveness, people have to stop telling lies and start telling the truth.

4. Give space in relationships. Not allowing others to be themselves, exactly as they are, kills relationships. This is because the "change" factor prevents the relationship from maturing. People must learn to leave space around their relatives, lovers, friends, etc., so they can be who they are.

5. Take responsibility. The biggest problem in

most people's lives is that they are unwilling to take responsibility for themselves. They are constantly pushing it off onto other people. This is probably the biggest part of "Getting It" in the est training. If the individual is not willing to take personal responsibility for himself, he should certainly not expect anyone else to take on this role.

Once the individual is willing to take on responsibility for himself, everything else in his life can begin to work. Ironically, according to est, most people have never taken or are not willing to take responsibility for themselves.

One of the most important things to "Get" is that the individual is fully responsible for his aliveness, and the world in which he lives. This means that the blame must be taken off of others and accepted by the individual. It means completing relationships with parents and other important life figures, taking the responsibility for what happens in life, and then moving on from it.

6. Life is a game. Whatever is in life is as it is, and whatever isn't is that way, too.

As Werner says in his booklet of aphorisms: "Obviously the truth is what's so. Not so obviously, it's also so what." *

What Does est Do?

With the secretiveness that surrounds est—who actually owns it, what the trust is all about, what happens to all of the money—and the publicity that it has received, it appears that est is pulling in money faster than the thousands of volunteers can count it!

The sixty-hour training program costs $250 per person. If it weren't for the thousands of volunteers who devote multithousands of working hours free of charge, est says this price would not cover costs. They state that all of the Graduate Seminars and other events run at break-even or at a loss.

In addition, there are a number of programs that est funds completely or supports: The Lompoc Prison training program in California, a workshop at a school in Watts, training programs in underprivileged areas. The est Advisory Board, with a number of high-ranking business and professional people to its credit, counsels est on these programs and other types of expansion.

Some people think that other staff members are bilking est of its income. However, according to est, they receive relatively low salaries that range from about $10,000 to $48,000 per year. Less than 200 people, in all thirteen operational cities, receive any salary. Everyone else is a volunteer. And these volunteers accomplish massive amounts of work—from the telephone calls to potential trainees and the arranging of name tags, papers and chairs to the cleaning of toilets and sealing and stamping of envelopes for the constant mailings that go out from its offices.

est is a fascinating compilation of truths. It seems to have its inception in such disciplines as Scientology, Mind Dynamics, Silva Mind Control, Zen, Transcendental Meditation, Transactional Analysis, Freud, Jung, Esalen and others. Actually, the best way to describe it is to say that est has its beginnings in the endings of all of these teachings.

est has its basis in experience rather than in belief. This is a difficult concept for the non-estian to grasp. This simply means that a person's beliefs about reality may have nothing to do with what he or she is experiencing. People get stuck in the way they were (beliefs) rather than where they are right now (experiences). "The purpose of the training," states an official est release, "is to transform your ability to experience living so that the situations you have been trying to change or have been putting up with clear up just in the process of life itself." This may sound like a bunch of hogwash, but to most graduates, sixty hours of training makes it all very reasonable and entirely within grasp.

est strongly maintains that if the trainee believes that the experience he receives is going to be psychological or therapeutic in nature, then he is mistaken. est is a unique experience. It is born out of living. Its basis is that people are tired of life not providing them with those things that they want. For example, a man is passed over for a special promotion that he was expecting; a young woman watches "helplessly" as her fifth serious relationship in a row goes down the drain; or a housewife complains about the extra twenty-five pounds she has been carrying around for as many years; a migraine headache prevents the young executive from properly accomplishing his work quota. est is a means for people to be able to work themselves out of all the things that have been dragging them down.

est provides trainees with an opportunity to add another dimension of living to their lives. Summed up in a single word: "aliveness." But what is so special about the "aliveness" is that it is an individual experience. The trainee hand-tailors this dimension to his or her own needs and awareness.

What the trainee gets from est can go on and on forever. That is why most say that est is an experience and not a belief. (And this is what makes it very different from any of the other disciplines.) Whatever data the trainer provides will be individually interpreted by the trainee. That is part of "Getting It."

So, if what you are or what you are doing doesn't seem to be working for you anymore, then perhaps through est, you can unstick yourself from a lot of concepts that you have been *trying* to correct. Through est, you can "experience your problems and make them disappear." You can transform your ability to experience living and clear up difficulties in your life.

A tall order for two weekends? Not so, according to graduate estians.

CHAPTER II

est ... It's a Long Way from the Restaurant Business

At the center of est is a powerful man by the name of Werner Erhard. Worshiped by much of his staff, he was originally christened Jack Paul Rosenberg, in Pennsylvania in 1935. Werner Hans Erhard founded est and is its chairman. The son of a family-style restaurant operator of middle-class background, he graduated from high school in 1952. That ended his formal education. He married soon after his graduation, and within eight years had four children to his credit. During that time, he worked at odd jobs, which included working in a meat-packing plant and as a supervisor in the construction business.

Werner Erhard, The Guru of est

About 1960, Jack packed his bags and left his home with his lady friend, Ellen, who later became his second wife. He made his way to St. Louis. To assure that he could not be traced, he changed his name. As a result of reading an article, he renamed himself Werner Hans Erhard.

Under that pseudonym, he spent the next few years as a sales representative, working for various self-improvement schools. In 1963, he joined the Parents Cultural Institute as an executive. This organization published a variety of materials for child development. There is much speculation that his actual duties were to hire, train and supervise door-to-door salesmen.

Werner's next job was with Grolier Society, Inc. A subsidiary of Grolier, Inc., this business division specialized in the sale of encyclopedias. This was done through home visits by the sales reps, and with considerable pressure applied to the buyer, so the story goes. Accordingly, Werner has been accused of training the demons who went out on the streets to peddle the wares of Grolier.

In 1971, he left Grolier Society to begin est.

During the period shortly before he began est, and while he was still involved with Grolier, Werner studied a number of different disciplines: Scientology, Mind Dynamics, and Silva Mind Control, to name a few. Leaders and believers at all of these organizations make claim that Werner has taken much of their material. And maybe that's true. But with a very big difference. Werner took the *experience*, and not the understanding.

Werner's salary, claimed at many different levels, not including fringe, is now generally accepted to be at $48,000 annually. In addition, he owns a Mercedes-Benz, a beautiful and expensive home high in the hills of Marin County, a private plane, and has three more children from his second wife. (Let it not be overlooked that Werner now claims the responsibility for his first wife and four children who have all been through the est training.) Volunteers at est act as his personal valet, chauffeur, housekeeper, etc.

There is much fanfare in the media over Werner's salary and benefits. Yet, the fact remains that Werner has the right to make money. Our system of free enterprise provides for it. And in fairness to him, the Public Information Office at est states that Werner's car was a gift from his family, and the home in Marin County was not from est.

The Sub-Gurus of est

The president of est is a former soda-pop man turned sub-guru. Don Cox, formerly general manager of the Coca Cola Bottling Company of California, took a considerable cut in salary to join est. After taking the training under Werner, he became an enthusiastic convert. Another credential that Mr. Cox boasts is his professorship at Harvard Business School.

est has a healthy Advisory Board to its credit. These are all people who have been through the training and have gotten value from it. As a result, they advise est on its new programs and charitable functions. The Advisory Board is as follows:

Phillip R. Lee, M.D.—Dr. Lee is both a physician and former chancellor of the University of California.

Frank M. Berger, M.D.—Dr. Berger is a professor of psychiatry at the University of Louisville School of Medicine. He is probably best known as the discoverer of the widely prescribed tranquilizer, Meprobamate.

George Brecher, M.D.—Dr. Brecher is a physician and a medical school professor.

James Bush, D.S.W.—Dr. Bush is a psychotherapist and a member of the faculty at Charles R. Drew Medical School.

Enoch Callaway, M.D.—Dr. Callaway is a professor of psychiatry at the University of California School of Medicine.

Ted Connolly—He is president of Connolly Development Inc., but is best known as the former all-pro ballplayer.

Don Cox—He is president and chief executive officer of est, and he is the former vice-president and director of planning for Coca Cola. He has also taught at Harvard Business School and holds a Doctorate of Business Administration.

John Crittenden—He is a writer and film critic.

John Denver—Mr. Denver is the pop musician, entertainer and composer.

Byron Eliashof, M.D.—He is a psychiatrist and a member of the faculty of the University of Hawaii Medical School.

John Emery, M.D.—He is a physician and plastic surgeon.

Douglas Engelbart, Ph.D.—He is a researcher and director of a research center at the Stanford Research Institute.

Werner Erhard—He is the founder of est.

Donald L. Fink, M.D.—He is a physician and professor of medicine at the University of California.

Charles H. Herbert, Jr., Ph.D.—He is president of Chess & Associates Educational Systems & Services, and associate director of Teacher Corps, University of California.

David C. Jacobsen, Th.M.—He is leader of the Prayer Renewal Workshop, and formerly served as a pastor at the Sausalito Presbyterian Church, Sausalito, California, and as a faculty member at the San Francisco Theological Seminary.

Robert Larzelere, M.D.—Dr. Larzelere is the manager of the Well-Being Department, est, and formerly a faculty member at the School of Medicine, University of California.

Peter Lenn, Ph.D.—He is president of the American Analysis Corporation, Inc., and board member of the Independent Learning Institute. He also devotes voluntary time to the field of education.

Theodore H. Long, Esq.—An est trainer, Mr. Long is manager, Seminar Department, est, manager, Communications Workshop Department, est, and formerly a councilman and vice-mayor in California.

F. Pearl McBroom, M.D.—Presently in private practice, Dr. McBroom was formerly a research consultant, Department of Psychiatry, Martin

Luther King Hospital, and a board member, Frederick Douglas Medical Center.

Helen Nahm, RN, Ph.D.—She is a registered nurse and dean emeritus, School of Nursing, University of California. She was also formerly a consultant to the WHO, Geneva, and the recipient of honorary degrees there.

Nguyen Nguyen, D.D.S.—Dr. Nguyen is chairman, Department of Endodontics, School of Dentistry, University of California. He is presently a consultant for the United States Air Force and Army Dental Corps and is the founder of Northern California Academy of Endodontics.

William Pack, Esq.—He is chairman, United Penta, Inc. and Telos, Inc.

F. Petrocelli—He is editor, Health Policy Program, School of Medicine, University of California and staff assistant to chancellors at the University of California.

Marcia Seligson—She is a writer and author and contributing editor, *New Times* Magazine.

Eugene C. Stevens—He is the mayor of Lompoc, California and faculty member and director of public relations, Allan Hancock College, California.

Fredrica Teer—He is a consultant for the New York State Division for Youth, National Black Theatre, Inc. and formerly a faculty member, School of Social Welfare, University of California.

John A. F. Wendt, Jr., Esq.—He is a judge in Pitkin County, Colorado and co-founder and former president, Bar Association of Pitkin County.

Leo Zeff, Ph.D.—A psychotherapist, Dr. Zeff is also a consultant in drug abuse and alcoholism and formerly the head psychologist at Oklahoma State Reformatory.

est denies that it has any connection with hypnosis, meditation, encounter groups, Eastern or Western cults, therapy, or psychology. As a matter of fact, only a tiny percentage of the est trainers have any psychological training at all.

The trainers, dedicated superstars who are put through the training under Werner himself, have backgrounds ranging from the medical profession (Jerry Joiner was formerly an obstetrician before joining est) to teacher (Landon Carter taught in India before he came into the est organization).

Werner's first trainer was a man named Stewart Emery. He originally worked with Werner while he was associated with Alexander Everett of Mind Dynamics. In the March 19, 1976 issue of *New Times* Magazine, there is an article dealing with Werner and est.

According to the article, Werner used his time at Mind Dynamics to train people for the seminar training, which he was preparing. Stewart Emery was offered a job as trainer at est's inception. He turned it down based on the fact that he felt that Werner was asking for too much personal dedication and not enough devotion to the concept of the est training. A number of months later, he decided that what Werner had put together was indeed a good thing, and joined the Organization.

The second time, Werner made the offer to Stewart less palatable, according to the *New Times* article. The finances of the offer were considerably less than the previous offer (although that offer is not precisely known), and Werner made it clear to Stewart that his purpose must be to serve Werner. Stewart could have none of his own beliefs. In spite of this, Stewart did join Werner and worked with him until recently when he left to start his own human potential movement, Actualizations.

The *New Times* article is particularly interesting in terms of revealing Werner's need for absolute and total devotion from his staff and volunteers. For example, if an est staff member wishes to have sex with another staff member, and he or she is married, Werner must have a note from the nonparticipating partner stating that it is okay for the spouse to have sex with the other est person. However, if est work doesn't go well, Werner assumes it is because of the extramarital activities and, therefore, one of the members must be relieved from the job. Nonmarried staff are allowed to have sex with whomever they please, *except* for est staff with whom they work directly.

This example of sexual discipline among est staff seems to be typical of the control Werner exercises over his employees and volunteers. According to the *New Times* article, est staff and volunteers confirm that Werner does require total and absolute dedication, "above and beyond the call of duty."

What Graduate estians Say About est

est is so heavily based in the individual experience that it would be superhuman not to question its validity.

Does it really work? Does it change your life around—even if you sleep through the entire training? Here's what a few of the grads had to say:

> "For the first time in my life, I realized that *I* created the migraine headache that cripples me at least one day each week. I'd chosen to give myself that experience as a way of getting even with my family for not taking enough responsibility for their lives. Now I seldom get even a minor headache."

> "For years I've been overweight. I'd come home to my apartment after work and stuff myself with goodies. Afterward, I'd hate myself and tears lulled me to sleep every night. For the first time in my life, I realized that I ate myself to sleep so that I wouldn't have to get in touch with how lonely I was. Today, I'm a size eight and when I'm lonely, it's because I've chosen to be that way."

> "I was scared to death to be alone. I thought that that was what I wanted. It was a great way to generate sympathy for poor me. Now that I know what I am doing to myself, it's much easier for me to correct the situation. I feel a lot more positive about myself, and I'm not afraid to be alone."

A behavioral study was done recently by a psychological testing company with specific reference to personality changes in people who had completed the est training. Results showed that measurable changes occurred, specifically in the area of improved self-image. Women demonstrated a greater variety of change than men. The explanation for this seems to be that the training helps to connect one with her feelings of self-esteem, an area where females certainly rate lower than males.

A tremendous amount has been written about est: articles, transcripts of television interviews, books, etc. Much of the information that has been spoken or printed is contradictory. The purpose of this book, therefore, will be to tear back some of the mystery that surrounds est and to reveal the est Organization (staff and volunteers), the training, and the language of est. Further on in this book, there is a chapter dealing with questions about est. The questions have been asked many times before at the est seminars and trainings, but most often the answers are such that they are not fully understandable or descriptive enough to the trainee or layperson. Therefore, you will find in that chapter that the answers deal with detailed explanations, rather than repeating what a trainer or staff member has said. These answers are designed to provide true insight into est, rather than "sell" the course, which many people feel est tries to do.

CHAPTER III

Glossary of est Words and Phrases

Unlike most books, the glossary for this book appears in the beginning. There is a very specific reason for this. The est training uses a lot of language which is unique to the training. Ordinary, commonplace words, with which everyone is familiar, take on a different meaning with est.

Therefore, do not read through the remainder of the book until you have had a chance to read this chapter. It is essential to the total understanding of everything that est is about. More importantly, there is much information in this book that will be misinterpreted by the reader if he does not understand the language of est.

Due to the specific meanings of many of the words, it will probably be necessary for the reader to refer back to this chapter during the reading of this book. What happens during the est training is, at times, very vague, at best. The purpose of this glossary, then, is to assist you in the total understanding of the training, so that you can "Get It."

acknowledge. This word has two definite meanings in est. The first, and most commonly used, is as a means of recognizing an individual or a point of view. ("I acknowledge what you have just said.") The second use of the word is as a thank you. This is done *without* making value judgments.

act. This is the social self. This is the front that we put on for society. This word is very important in the est training, since it is believed that everyone "puts on an act." People get along in society because they don't "call one another on each other's acts." The purpose of the est training is to get rid of your "act" and accept the real you.

agreement. This word has two interpretations. The ground rules for est training are also referred to as agreements. In everyday usage, it is the understanding between individuals as to a method of action. One of the tenets of est is that life doesn't work because people are constantly breaking agreements.

alive. This is a statement of life. It means to be fully accepting of self and aware of the choices that can be made in living.

aliveness. This means awareness. It is living life to the fullest extent. Aliveness is a direct result of alive in the estian sense of the term.

and. This means as a result of. It is always used in the positive sense of the term. For example, "I have to go to the store and I choose not to." Using the word "and" allows people to get in touch with their choices. This word almost always replaces the usage of "but."

and that's okay. This usually indicates a difference of opinion between two or more parties, but allows for the choice by the parties. "And" is used in the positive sense. By replacing it with the word "but," it takes the guilt out of the phrase and allows for another individual to have his or her own feelings.

asshole. This word is a tenet of est. The training is based on the fact that all trainees are assholes, *i.e.*, machines or tubes. One gives up his asshole status when one gives up his "acts" or social self. Usually, it is the objective of an est trainee to get rid of his asshole status, which can only be done when he recognizes that he is an asshole.

assist. This is another extremely important word in the est language. It replaces the word "help." Assisting allows an individual to support another individual without taking away his or her responsibility, and assist can only be made if the first individual could function without the support of the other. Assist also has a close relationship to the word volunteer.

barrier. This word has two meanings. It is an immaterial obstruction, which the individual uses as a means of preventing himself from accomplishing a job, project, etc. In the second sense of the word, it is an obstruction or obstructions that all trainees have in their minds before entering the training. Part of the purpose of the training is to break down these obstructions or barriers in order to get at the true self.

being right is costing you your life. This means that it is more important to "win" than it is to be in touch with what the individual is feeling. Being right is closely integrated into all our "acts." Part of the purpose of the est training is to break away from this sense of being right.

belief. This is the act of placing trust or confidence in a concept or conviction and accepting it as Truth. Beliefs prevent an individual from experiencing life. As a result, the individual experiences life incorrectly, since the experiences are based on beliefs, which are unTruths.

but. This word is almost never used in the est language except to tell individuals that its use should be avoided. The word "and" replaces "but." Its meaning is negative and implies lack of results. It prevents individuals from making choices.

buttons. These are negative-response mechanisms that trigger an automatic response in the individual. This response is based on experiencing the past (with its beliefs and barriers) rather than living in the present.

cause. That which produces a result or a consequence. When an individual works from cause (experience), he accepts responsibility for his actions.

center. This exists inside the individual and is created by the individual under the guidance of the est trainer. The center is similar to an "inner room" where the individual can safely deal with problems that he or she might have. The individual can "bring" people into this center and discuss those things of importance to the individual.

change. This is a useless word in est language, since by changing or altering something, it still remains with the individual. The purpose of est training is not to change those things the individuals have been putting up with, but to "disappear" them.

choice. This is the act of consciously selecting. In order to be able to choose, an individual must take responsibility for his or her life. If an individual is coming from a position of responsibility, situations that he or she have been trying to change will clear up and choices can then be made. This word has two meanings. Most commonly, it is used instead of the words "understandable" and "open." The second meaning of this word is in terms of an individual being free from guilt or uncertainty.

complete. This is very much an estian word. It means wholly finished. Relationships, for example, must be completed in order to clear up life's situations.

considerations. This is a very commonly used word in est. These are the reservations, unanswered questions, judgments, beliefs, etc., which still exist and, as a result, prevent the individual from experiencing the moment. Considerations must be cleared up before an individual can experience a situation.

create. This means to bring about, to cause, to originate. According to est, an individual creates everything in his or her life, including all sicknesses, accidents, pleasant and unpleasant situations.

data. Data is information. Part of the purpose of the est training is to provide individuals with a tremendous amount of data.

disappear it. By experiencing a situation, and not just understanding or believing in it, one moves past "changing it" and removes it from one's life. Disappearing a situation enables an individual to transform his or her life by clearing it up.

dumping. This term simply means complaining.

effect. This is an est word meaning "out of control." An individual at the effect of a situation is letting that situation run or victimize him. The only way out of effect is to choose it and then it will disappear.

esthole. This is the estian equivalent of an asshole or machine. Generally, it is used to describe a person possessed by an excessive and irrational zeal for est.

experience. This is recreating a situation and feeling it rather than knowing or believing in it. When an individual fully experiences a situation, he or she relives it.

for sure. That's correct. Certainly. Of course. This is the equivalent of an est slang word.

get in touch with. This is simply experiencing what is going on with you. It means removing barriers to get at the experience.

get off it. This usually means to call an individual

on his "act." It is a phrase used to make an individual aware of his asshole status.

Getting It.   This has many different meanings. It is the purpose of the est training. It can mean anything from "nothing" to "something." It is an individual experience. One only "Gets It" out of experience, never out of understanding or belief.

good.   It is noncommittal acknowledgment that a statement has been heard. Often, it means that the individual who has heard the statement does not actually agree with it but acknowledges your right to say it.

go to the beach.   This is a private place in the mind of the trainee or graduate, reached through a process. Generally, it is a relaxing beach, created by the individual, as a place of safety and tranquility.

help.   This is the act of taking away responsibility from another individual. When an individual is "helped" as opposed to "assisted," it is an admission that he or she is incapable of accomplishing the act alone. According to est, helping should be avoided.

intention.   This is a plan of purpose or action. It is used instead of "trying," since this is a nonhyphen word. One's intentions are always accomplished.

love.   Love means accepting another individual exactly as he or she is and giving the space to be that way. It means choosing the individual as he or she is.

notice.   This is a means of calling an individual's attention to another point of view. By having an individual notice another individual's point of view, the need to be "right" is replaced by a positive action.

observe.   This is to perceive a situation without the need to evaluate or judge it.

on purpose.   On line. On target. This means to achieve a goal without letting any other situation get in the way.

participation. This is to share in fully. It is the beginning of experience. It leads to completion.

pictures. Pictures are images in the mind. Pictures are based on belief systems. They tend to act as barriers.

point of view. Observations. Pictures. And considerations. Generally, it is a non-experiential action or idea. A point of view has the potential to be dangerous to an individual since it can create a barrier.

process. "A method by which a person experiences and looks at, in an expanded state of consciousness and without judgment, what is actually so with regard to specific areas in his or her life, and one's fixed or unconscious attitudes about those areas." (Definition is from the est brochure.) It is a method whereby one can get in touch with and fully experience situations, choose them, and make them disappear. In the est training, a process is achieved with the guidance of the trainer. Outside of the est training, the process is often a fantasy or meditative experience.

push your buttons. This is being out of control. Another individual pushes your buttons. It is an automatic response based on past non-experience and the individual's reaction always resembles the past situation.

racket. This is closely related to the "act." It is automatic behavior based on past non-experience. Individuals "run a racket" because they think it will get them what they want.

reality. Self-actualization. Enlightenment. Experience.

reasons. Reasons are excuses or justifications for actions. Reasons are generally used as a means of avoiding responsibility and not choosing.

resist. This is the opposite of choosing. When you resist a situation, you are out of control, and a situation runs you. You must choose a situation in order to be able to disappear the resistance.

responsibility.   This means the ability to act out of one's own experience. It has nothing to do with blame or guilt or burden. Before one can choose life, one has to take responsibility for it.

running your life.   This means being out of control. Self-victimization.

share.   To participate. To communicate. This is an estian word that is always used in the positive sense. If one complains, one is not "sharing" but is "dumping" instead. Dumping is something to be avoided. Sharing leads to experience.

source.   In estian language, it is always used as a verb and it means to create, as in "I sourced my new job."

space.   This word has two meanings according to est training. In the first meaning, space is something that you have inside of you. It is a means to reaching your center. During a process, by getting in touch with your spaces, it enables an individual to relax, get past barriers, and to experience. In the second definition, space is allowing for observation; *i.e.*, making no evaluations or judgments. It has nothing to do with distance. Giving an individual space takes away the resistance.

stuck.   This is being unable to get out of. Being stuck is a barrier to experience. One is stuck in a point of view. One can only get unstuck by choosing it and disappearing it.

truth.   This is the same as experience. Truth is the opposite of a lie, and means to understand or believe something.

try.   Try is a nonword. You either do or you don't. Trying keeps the individual from experiencing.

unconscious.   This means to become unaware, close

out. Individuals constantly "go unconscious" as a way of avoiding choice or responsibility.

understanding. Understanding means a lie . . . the opposite of the truth. Understanding prevents an individual from experiencing.

unstuck. Getting away from resistance. Getting unstuck enables an individual to move toward experience. The next positive step after becoming unstuck is to observe.

upset. An upset is an unpleasant situation. Upsets must be experienced so they can be disappeared. Upsets are dangerous because they have the potential to control or run your life.

value. To value is to regard highly.

what's coming up for you. This is getting past the barriers and becoming in touch with what's going on with the individual. What's coming up is one of the necessary steps toward experiencing.

yama, yama. This means blah, blah. Etc., etc. It usually indicates meaningless conversation.

CHAPTER IV

The Guest Seminar

There are two types of Guest Seminars that est runs. The first is a Guest Seminar held in a large commercial hotel, and it is exclusively for people who have never attended the est training. The second kind of Guest Seminar is one that is held in conjunction with an est event. For example, est graduates are allowed (and definitely encouraged) to bring guests to the Post-Graduate Training Seminar. However, the guests remain with the graduates for only a short period of time before the guests move to another room for their own mini-Seminar.

Generally speaking, guests come to these Seminars for three reasons:

1. They are recruited by friends who have been to the est training and want them to share the experience.
2. A small portion of them come after reading articles about est, from which they conclude that the training can help them.
3. Some people have heard about est through the

media and other sources and come to the Seminars out of pure curiosity.

The number of people attending a Guest Seminar can range anywhere from ten to five hundred people.

Guests at the Seminar tend to be familiar-looking people, *i.e.*, a cross section of middle America. Both sexes are equally represented. Although there are always a few longhairs in the crowd, most guests are professionals, executives, housewives, etc. (the same type who eventually join the est training).

The Seminars always start promptly on time. The Guest Seminars (or portions for the guests of graduates) are run by leaders—or est trainers—who have been especially trained by Werner to answer questions about est.

The purpose of the Guest Seminar, according to est, is to clear up questions and considerations about est and decide if the training is something in which a guest would like to participate. More simply stated, its purpose is to bring an individual to choice about taking the training. "Choice," as described in the glossary, is est lingo for "making a decision."

The Seminar leader gives a briefing on some of the things that happen in the est training. He describes a little of the sharing experiences. (Sharing is simply audience participation, whereby an experience or thought is shared with others on a *voluntary* basis. Guests and trainees are always assured that they never have to share anything unless they *choose* to.)

There is also a brief description of the Processes. These Processes are a very important part of the est training, according to the leader, and they really can't be described. (Author's note: A brief description of a Process is an exercise, which takes place with your eyes closed, whereby you look inside yourself and experience what is going on for you. You don't do this by yourself; you are guided by your trainer, who gives you specific thoughts with which to deal, or brings forth specific images.) The Processes are exercises that enable you to go beyond the belief and concepts on which you so heavily rely, and experience what is happening with you. The Processes help to experience the moment.

Part of the Guest Seminars deal with the leaders sharing their personal experiences within the training. Werner forbids them to actually describe the training, but the leaders are encouraged to share their experiences. The stories related by the leaders are typical of life and living—dissatisfaction with a job, boss, or marriage; loneliness; living in the future; living in the past; loving someone who doesn't return the love. The leaders share that during the est training they got in touch with what was running their lives. By experiencing it and acknowledging it, the leaders were able to clear up situations that they had not been able to clear up previously. In so doing, they took responsibility for their individual lives. (This is a basic est tenet.)

The leaders share their experiences with the guests who are usually very intrigued by the transformations that have been related to them. As a result, during the guest participation or sharing time, the leaders are deluged with questions about est. How does it work? What makes it work? Can it work for them? The leaders are skilful in acknowledging the questions without ever really answering them.

In addition to the questions about est, there are the usual questions about not being able to go to the bathroom, to leave the room at all, to smoke in the training room, to talk, or to eat, except as specified by the trainer. (There is more about this in the chapter on Pre-Training.) The leaders explain that est trainees don't have to do anything that they do not choose to do. However, there are certain ground rules or agreements that are set up by est because they work, and therefore, they become the agreements to do the training. A trainee, at the beginning of the training, gets to choose whether or not he wishes to accept these agreements. If the answer is positive, then he or she proceeds with the training.

Next, the leaders cover some of the business end of est; for example, cost of the training, amount of deposit, length of the training, etc. After a brief discussion on the business aspect of est, there is a break. At this point, est staff and volunteers make a massive effort to get guests to sign up for the training.

It is a high-pressure effort worthy of any door-to-door encyclopedia sales team. (Ex-est volunteers will often relate that there is a terrific amount of pressure laid on them to get guests signed up into est. Volunteers are told that all life situations are created by them, including their ability to obtain registrations. If enough people weren't signing up, it was their fault because they created it. If the volunteers created a negative selling situation, then they should recognize that and change it.)

It is often stated by guests that est staff and volunteers become like aggressive animals on the break, doing almost anything to obtain a registration. The purpose behind the effort, according to est, is supposedly to bring people to decision about the training. Time and again, guests complain about the pressure techniques. est personnel apply so much pressure that many guests turn off on est.

As a result of the sales effort, there is frequently much anger and hostility among the crowd. After the break, it is common that the sharing is taken up primarily with the rage people feel about the pressure that has been applied to them. In one Seminar, guests were so angry that the entire time left was devoted to this subject.

Many people say that they would never have gone through the training after attending a Guest Seminar if they hadn't *previously* made up their minds. Est maintains they are only bringing people to choice and that the guests are rebelling against responsibility.

Graduates are urged to bring guests to Seminars. Often, the grads are made to feel that they won't be able to get their full experience from the training if they don't convince others to share the experience. Graduates who do enthusiastically bring friends are often in for a big shock by their reactions. Many guests have been known to have "bad experiences" at the Seminars. Or even worse, they become angry with their friends who persuaded them to attend. (For example, a businessman attended the est training and got a great deal of value from it. It was important to him that his partner share the experience. Not only could the other partner get a lot of value from it, he thought, but it would be a shared experience that would bring them closer together. The partner went and came away from the Guest Seminar appalled by the selling techniques. He never signed up for est. As a result, est is now a barrier between the two men.)

People who have attended a Guest Seminar or other est Seminars in which guests are allowed to participate seldom come forth to speak out about the value he or she received in the Guest Seminar. Almost always, there will be heated, negative feelings in existence about the pressure applied to sign up. Yet, a tremendous number of people sign up for the training as a result of the high-pressure sales job.

It is an interesting question to pose as to why

thousands of people sign up for the est training as a result of these Guest Seminars when they are so thoroughly turned off by the selling techniques. The answer seems to lie in the very foundations of what est is all about. And that is responsibility. People are not willing to take responsibility for themselves, according to est staff. They don't want to choose. When someone else brings them to choice (such as an est volunteer), it drives them crazy. Ironically, the very things about which they are screaming, *i.e.*, responsibility, the right to live and experience, to choose life, not to resist it, is exactly the reason as to why these people flock to est in droves.

Guests attend the Seminars for a number of reasons, such as their friends persuaded them, or intriguing articles. Although they are aggravated by the selling techniques deep down, most of the people have a genuine desire to find out about themselves and to change themselves in some manner. Ironically, this desire to change is in exact opposition to the basic tenets of est. And, this desire to change can be best typified by some examples of dialogue between guests.

"My best friend divorced her husband after fifteen years of marriage. She says est gave her the courage to do it. I hope that I can either get myself together and improve my marriage or get the hell out of it."

"My wife told me that if I didn't attend a Seminar and sign up for est that she would divorce me. I still haven't made up my mind."

"My son went through the training. Then my wife. I can't believe the changes in both of them. I hope I can get some of whatever 'it is.'"

"I heard that est is a great place to casually meet men. You can kind of look them over here and see what the pickings are."

"My boyfriend had a real problem with his own feelings of self-worth. Now he seems to feel good about himself. He says it's all a result of the est experience. My life could run better. Maybe it will."

When the guest sharing has been completed after the break, the Seminars are generally concluded with a pep talk from the leader about the opportunity everyone present has to make something of his or her life. The est training will allow them to "Get" the ways to make life turn out perfectly. It is a promise that is difficult to turn away from. And that promise of eternal bliss is probably more responsible for guests signing up for the training than the real est tenet: taking responsibility for life.

CHAPTER V

The Pre-Training Seminar

The purpose of the Pre-Training Seminar, which is a three-and-one-half-hour session held on a weeknight prior to the first weekend, is to acquaint trainees with the following:

1. Background on est. The Seminar Leader provides a minimal amount of information on the subject. At the time of presentation, it all seems to make perfectly good sense. Upon reflection, it seems to leave all the questions still unanswered. During the "sharing" (audience participation), many questions are asked about est. For example, "Why does the training cost $250?" The answer: "Because that's what it costs." Or, "Why can't I go to the bathroom except on a break?" The answer: "Because that's what works."

2. The ground rules of est. They are basically:
   a. There is to be no gum, candy, cookies, or food of any kind in the training room.

43

    b. There are to be no timepieces in the training room.

    c. Note-taking and recordings of the est training are forbidden.

    d. There will be no food except on a food break.

    e. There will be no urinating except on a bathroom break. This does not preclude that fact that a trainee can go to the bathroom in his/her pants or into a bag in the training room. (This was done during the training.) Also, there is no eating of any food whatsoever on a bathroom break. Trainees are allowed to use the phones.

    f. No smoking is allowed at any time in the training room.

    g. During the period from the first Saturday to the last Sunday (nine consecutive days), there will be no drugs, sleeping pills, alcohol, grass, or medicine of any kind unless authorized by a doctor. Those people with a medical problem, which includes special medicines, eating habits, specific exercises, etc., are seated in the back row so they can be informed by est staff or volunteers when it is time to care for themselves.

    h. There is to be no "busy work" allowed in the training room, such as knitting, reading, doodling, etc.

    i. During the training, there is to be no work or communication with other disciplines, *e.g.*, no Zen, TM, Zazen, or Rolfing.

3. The search for enlightenment. The Seminar

leader provides a minimal amount of information on the need to realize self-actualization, or enlightenment. This is done through the experience of est, rather than the belief in a concept or theory with which est might provide the trainee.

In addition, est is not recommended for persons who have been hospitalized for emotional disorders. If the trainee is in therapy, or has been in therapy within the last six months and is not/was not winning in therapy, then it is recommended that the trainee *not* take the training. If a trainee who is not winning decides to take the training, a note from his therapist is required stating that the therapist will be available for consultation during the training period.

In order to more clearly understand what happens at an est Pre-Training Seminar, it is necessary to share my experience of it and what others, with whom I have spoken, say about it.

Our leader's name was Marvin. He was tall and slender with a closely cropped beard and short hair, well dressed (a copy of Werner's style, a trademark of nearly all the male est staff), but cocky, I thought.

As soon as he spoke, I began to dislike him. He talked on and on. And as he spoke, I began to realize why I disliked him so intensely. His language was totally estian. "Got It." "Good." "For sure." "And that's okay." "It's running your life." "That's your racket." "My intention is. . . ." It seemed to me that he had forgotten the English language as we know it. Not only that, but I also realized that he spoke exactly like one of my friends who had been through the training. The same inflections, everything. Why can't they talk like regular people, I wondered, instead of making up another language?

When Marvin finished with all of the ground rules, the discussion was opened to audience participation in order to answer any questions or considerations that we might still have. Immediately, hands shot up.

Q. "What if we get sick to our stomachs if we don't eat for a long time?"
A. "Experience your sickness. Thank you."

Q. "Can we take our birth control pills?"
A. "Yes. We want the same number of people finishing the training as started it." (Laughter)

Q. "What happens if we have to go to the bathroom before an announced break?"
A. "You get to experience having to go to the bathroom, and you don't go."

Q. "Marvin, I think you're an asshole."
A. "Thank you."

Q. "What happens if going to the bathroom isn't usually a problem, but suddenly we have to go?"
A. "Experience it."

Q. "Can we bring cough drops into the training room?"
A. "Not unless you have a note from your doctor requiring you to take them."

Q. "Another bladder question. I just had the flu and drank a lot of liquids. What if I really have to go before a break?"
A. "Be with that feeling."

Q. "Can I bring a pillow to the training?"
A. "Yes."

On and on the questions went. The answers varied very little. It seemed that every variety of bladder question was asked. The majority of trainees seemed to be obsessed by the fact that they would be unable to go to the bathroom at will.

After reviewing the ground rules of est, we were told that they were to be our agreement with est. We didn't have to do any of those things. That was our choice to make. But given the choice, if we accepted those ground rules as a prerequisite to the training, then we were expected to stick by them.

When people asked why we had to do all those nonsensical things, Marvin told us, "Because Werner found it works."

And, strangely enough, it does work. During the first weekend, I resented not being able to leave the room at will, or to eat at my convenience. But after twelve hours of staying awake, listening to data and not being able to get away from myself, I realized how much I "go unconscious" and avoid those things that are coming up for me. (Suddenly, I realized how often in my therapy sessions I would put a barrier between myself and a problem I didn't want to face on the rationalization that the session was almost over.) It greatly intensified my feelings when I was not able to escape from them. However, when Marvin droned on about all these ground rules in the Pre-Training, boring me half to death, it didn't seem so reasonable or purposeful.

In spite of the fact that much fanfare is made about trainees being locked in a room, the experience of being kept behind closed doors can be an invaluable part of the training. (It should be remembered that the trainee remains there by choice.) Trainees are kept in a closed room because it works. It's part of the ground rules and, therefore, an agreement on the part of the trainees. (There is much discussion about the "trainee prisoner." The practice is often referred to as a means of "brainwashing." However, it should be noted that the purpose of brainwashing is to change entirely, or to alter, basic belief systems.) est does not try to change the trainee in any way. Werner believes that all people are perfect the way they are. Unfortunately, research shows that the concept of perfection is a difficult thing for most people to accept.

There is no composite of the "typical estian." However, the majority is middle or upper-middle class. Trainees are young and old, rich and not poor, employed and unemployed, married, divorced, single and from every walk of life. A sizable number of the trainees have never been in therapy.

Most of the trainees attend est because they have been recruited by friends who have experienced est and are enthusiastic about it. Others attend because of articles or programs they have read or seen. A few sign up because they have heard about it by word of mouth.

Celebrities rave about it. Although it is officially denied by the est organization, former staff members and volunteers say that VIP's are given special treatment to insure that their experience is a meaningful one. This is done because celebrities have the potential to provide a tremendous amount of free public relations for est. Additionally, a celebrity who raves about est publicly is bound to generate many new trainees and converts. (After experiencing est, John Denver wrote a song about it.)

I had come to est as a result of my friends and

business acquaintances taking the training. Although all of them had passed on glowing recommendations about est, I was still skeptical. Life has never seemed that easy to me, and I just couldn't quite accept all the marvelous life changes they were so dramatically describing to me. Indeed, Marvin was describing est as an experience that would "turn our lives around, 180 degrees. We could sleep through the entire training," he told us, "and we would still 'Get It.'" I couldn't conceive that anything quite so earth shattering as that could possibly happen to us while we were asleep!

I am basically an optimistic person, and so I was anxious to find out if there was any truth to all that I had been hearing. However, Marvin was certainly not doing anything to establish positive (and believable) feelings toward est on my part. I think that the real incentive behind my attending the first weekend was that I had *previously* made up my mind to go and that est *already* had my $250.

In order to enroll in the est program, I was required to fill out an application form with basic information about myself (name, address, etc.) and a statement of the specific goals and achievements I desired from the training. The completed application was sent in with my $30 deposit, in advance of the Pre-Training Seminar.

On the evening of the Seminar, which is held in a hotel similar or identical to the ones where the training is held, I was greeted by a smiling, frozen-faced volunteer. She asked me my last name and then directed me to the proper table where I could pick up my name tag. This tag is required in order to gain admittance to the training room.

It hadn't been my kind of day at the office, so I wasn't really surprised when my turn came and they told me that, before they could issue me my name tag, I had to clear up some questions they still had about me. It turned out that my application had been rejected for "nonspecific" information. I'm a business executive. I had paid $250 of my hard-earned money to take the training. I felt as if I really didn't need that kind of grief. (There had been a terrific snow-storm in New York that day, and the city was paralyzed. I had put an amazing amount of energy into just getting to the hotel. To be harassed about an insignificant application form seemed somehow irrelevant in light of the effort I had put into getting there, *and getting there on time.*)

My specific goal answer had been rejected because I put down, "I don't have any." At the time, I thought that made perfectly good sense: it would enable me to take the training with an open mind. After rewriting the paragraph twice, my answer was finally accepted. (How was I to know that it would be rejected again upon review by the Registrar, and that I would have to rewrite it once more the following Saturday!)

However, for the time being, my application had gained acceptance and I had been issued a name tag as my reward. My first name was spelled in big, bold Magic Marker-type letters, with my last name discreetly printed underneath it.

est is a stickler on detail. I met a man at est whose name tag read: Den. He had been christened Dennis, but his friends called him by the shortened version, and he preferred it. During a part of the est training, everyone is required to fill out a Personality Profile Card. Den did this and signed his name, as is required. Later on, he was called aside for questioning as to why he had signed his name Dennis. (Apparently, they thought he might be an impostor!) We were all suitably impressed by this "catch" on the part of est.

The major emphasis of the Pre-Training Seminar is to provide trainees with data and to touch upon any considerations they might still have about the training.

Another important topic in the Pre-Training is the subject of enlightenment. Although most people are not terribly clear as to exactly what this is, enlightenment is an especially meaningful part of the overall training. Enlightenment is something the trainees are seeking.

The search for enlightenment is a direct result of the increased leisure time that is evident among the middle classes. As more time becomes available, and the pressure to survive lets up, people question the tragedies, complexities and uncertainties of life. Usually, this is not a comforting experience. As a result, people become disenchanted with their status quo existences. Instinctively, they begin to seek a better way, a way that will lead to the happiness and aliveness that they desire so much.

This search for a new and better way is reflected in the fact that Scientology, Silva Mind Control, TA, TM, Rolfing, Esalen, Yoga, Mortality Consciousness are not only commonplace dinner-party topics, but commonplace on advertising billboards as well. Books on self-improvement and pop-psychology are runaway best sellers. (A friend recently created mass panic in her conservative Wall Street office when co-workers thought she had suffered a coronary. Actually, she was meditating at the end of a long, tough day. A workoholic friend leaves his hectic public relations firm at 4:00 P.M. on weekdays to meet with his Zen master and to study the discipline.)

Suddenly, people are no longer weird or perverted if they confer with an astrologer before making an important date or decision. All of this seems to be linked to the pop-psych trips in which everyone clamors to take part. est is no exception. It represents an opportunity for an individual to partake in a revolutionary consciousness movement—the beginning of true self-experience, *i.e.*, enlightenment.

The Pre-Training Seminar is designed to impart the feeling that there is hope—an opportunity to climb aboard and share in life's self-actualization, enlightenment experience. The Seminar will leave the trainee confident that he is not a fool to seek the Truth (whatever that turns out to be in reality). This hope for enlightenment is mentioned by many during the sharing.

It is a commonplace thing to search to fulfill human potential. As soon as people get past the "need" stage in their lives (survival), and begin to recognize their "wants," the search for enlightenment becomes a never-ending process. Many say that est ends this search. The Pre-Training Seminar nurtured that hope.

The Pre-Training Seminar, then, basically provides trainees with some background on est, good coverage of the ground rules and agreements, audience sharing, and some data on enlightenment. In addition, the Seminar ends with a Process. According to an est brochure, this is "a method by which a person experiences and looks at, in an expanded state of consciousness and without judgment, what is actually so with regard to specific areas in his or her life, and one's fixed or unconscious attitudes about those areas." More simply and clearly put, it is an exercise where, under the direction of the leader, the bodies (and therefore the minds) of the trainees are relaxed. The leader then has each trainee think about different events in his or her life. For example, the trainees are told to think of a happy time, a sad time, a loving time, an angry time. The purpose of reflecting upon these images is to recreate them in the mind of the trainee as an experience of the memory. This Process is a simplified version of what the trainees experience a number of times during the training. This is discussed in detail in the chapter on training.

One last exercise, which is given to the trainees before the Pre-Training Seminar is concluded, is an assignment for the trainee to spend several hours (not necessarily consecutively) during the week examining his or her life in reverse order, as if it were on a movie projector. The trainee is to look at the images (memories) frame by frame, and experience them. There are always many questions about this exercise, but it is a relatively simple one. The purpose of the exercise is for the trainee to review his or her life, look at the images, and experience them.

The Seminar ends with specific instructions as to the hotel, address, date and time (8:30 A.M.) for the first day of the training. There is a general reminder of the ground rules and agreements, and a warning to observe them by choice. There is special emphasis about arriving on time at the training. Trainees were advised to be at the hotel earlier than 8:30 A.M., so that there would be time to pick up name tags and clear up any last-minute questions. Trainees are to be seated by 8:30 A.M., ready to begin the training. People who are late are not allowed into the training room until they take the responsibility for their lateness.

On that note, the trainees are released for the night.

CHAPTER VI

The First Seventeen Hours

The training *begins* on a Saturday at 8:30 A.M. This means that all trainees must have picked up their name tags, answered any last questions, gone to the bathroom, deposited all watches and food *outside* of the training room, and have been seated and ready to begin at 8:30 A.M. (Coordinating this kind of event with 250 people is no simple task. Yet it is constantly done, and done correctly each week.) Indeed, all the trainees are in their seats at the appointed hour. The few late stragglers are forced to wait outside the room until they have taken the responsibility for their lateness. It is a broken agreement and a serious infraction of the est training. Broken agreements, according to est staff, are what keep life from working.

The following is a typical, "first day" training session. The est training takes place in the same kind of hotel as the Pre-Training Seminar, in a room large enough to seat 250 people. As usual, all of the mirrors and paintings in the room are covered over. This is to prevent trainees from being distracted during the training. All of the chairs are perfectly aligned, with even amounts of space between the rows. The room is ice cold. Trainees are shivering from the chill. Those who have covered their name tags over with a sweater or coat, due to the cold, are reminded to keep their tags in full view.

A loud voice fills the room. A casually well-dressed, middle-aged man walks down the center aisle, giving instructions. Anyone who was relaxed, immediately sits up and pays attention to the assistant, who is now speaking at full volume. THERE WILL BE NO TALKING. For the next two hours, without a microphone or voice amplifier of any kind, he will cover the ground rules for the est training. (These are the same rules that were covered in the Pre-Training.) Everyone is informed that he or she will not be able to talk, smoke, eat, knit, take notes or move from the chair while in the training room. No one can leave the room unless a formal break is announced, and then the trainee can do only what is provided for on that break. For example, a bathroom break allows for no food, but certain fruit juices, coffee, tea, soda, etc. can be consumed. Telephone calls are allowed on any of the breaks.

During the course of the training, there are to be no drugs, alcohol, medicine (except under a doctor's orders) or use of other disciplines. This is part of the agreement that the trainees have with est.

Those people with a medical problem (and they were required to bring a note from their doctors, or to speak with staff prior to the start of the training) would sit in the back row at *all* times so that they could properly provide for themselves and not disturb other trainees. No one but the medically exempt could sit in the back row.

Furthermore, he boomed on, all trainees who are seated next to someone they knew prior to the training are required to move to another seat. Hands are raised in response to this order, and people are moved away from their friends and spouses. During the time of the training, trainees are never to sit next to someone they knew prior to the training. Nor are they ever to sit next to the same person twice during the training.

There are no timepieces and food allowed in the training room at any time. Although this had been covered a number of times, trainees are now told that, if they have watches, timepieces, food, candy, cookies, gum, etc. in the room, they should turn it in for checking with staff in the back of the room. For a moment, there is complete silence in the room. Then slowly, a few people stand up and start toward the back of the room. More follow. Several dozen in all make their way to the tables to unload all their goodies. (In my training, I had brought along some peanut-butter cookies into the room that I did not turn in. I couldn't bear the thought of standing up and identifying myself as the possessor of three cookies. I kept them with me until the first break, when I threw them away. However, I must say that when lunchtime passed with no food, and my stomach started to grumble, my mind wandered away from what the trainer was saying, and fantasized about the cookies!)

When the assistant had covered all the ground rules, time was provided to answer questions from the audience. Again, there was much obsession with the bathroom breaks, as well as questions pertaining to low-alcoholic beverages, e.g., beer, wine (not allowed), use of aspirin and other nonmedicine medicines. When these questions were over, and everyone finally believed that he or she could only leave the room on a formal break, the audience was reminded once again that timepieces and food were not allowed in the training room at any time. The assistant would provide one last opportunity for people to turn them in. Once again, trainees made their way to the back of the room. ("I can't believe this," I thought. "More people unloading watches and food. How ridiculous!" Then I remembered my three cookies with considerable guilt.)

When the ground rules were concluded, the assistant reminded everyone that these were agreements with est—not rules. Each trainee should recognize that he or she is *choosing* to accept these ground rules—they are not being enforced.

The final exercise before the training really begins is the review on exactly how to hold the microphone. During the sharing, if a trainee speaks, a microphone must be used so that the question or statement can be properly heard. This accomplished, everyone is directed to sit down.

Suddenly, a deep, massive voice is heard. Heads swing around to see a young, nicely dressed man stride across the room. Everyone faces front. The assistant is gone. Only the trainer remains with the 250, uncomfortable-looking people. He stands at the front of the room, with no microphone, and begins to address the audience. Looking like a military convert, he begins screaming. Swearing. Calling everyone assholes. Machines. Liars. Hopeless assholes, unable to make life work.

The trainer then described what the trainees would be feeling as the day moved on. They were told that every emotion would come up, and that most of the trainees would handle these emotions by "going unconscious." This would be accomplished through daydreaming, sleeping, fantasizing, etc. "Anything," he predicted, "to keep you from experiencing yourselves." However, he knowingly assured the trainees that, in spite of everything they would do to escape from themselves, before the training was over, they would "Get It."

The trainer's certainty begins to have its reaction among the crowd. There is shifting and squirming. And a few people are already sleeping.

Then he takes time out to warn the trainees that at times the room is going to get very noisy. *Very, very noisy.* You could see that the trainees were unsure of what he meant by this. Later on, the trainees found that during certain Processes, there would be a tremendous amount of screaming, moaning, crying, vomiting, etc. Indeed, the room does get very noisy. That's part of the training. The trainee is then instructed to take what he "Gets" and keep his "soles in the room." This has the effect of making people even more uncomfortable than they already are.

"You are confused. You are poor slobs. You are all so confused about life, so filled up with beliefs and concepts, that you don't even realize that you're fucking machines. Assholes. And you're here today because your life isn't working for you. All your deceptions and 'acts' haven't gotten you anywhere."

The attack continues. Hour after hour, the trainees are bombarded with this verbal flagellation. Before long, several people begin to cry. (Occasionally, someone throws up in the early stages of the training, but usually, this comes later.) There is no change in the trainer's manner.

"Your belief systems are all wrong. You're fucking up everything. The purpose of the training is to transform your ability to experience living so that the situations you have been trying to change or have been putting up with clear up just in the process of life itself."

The harangue still goes on. Generally, it is a combination of philosophy and filthy language, designed to confuse and scare the trainee, and most of all, to expose him to himself, as he really is.

A number of hours into the lecture, it becomes much more esoteric in nature. By the time the first break is announced, most of the trainees are totally unsure as to what is happening and why they are there.

Bathroom breaks never last more than thirty minutes. During that time, the trainee is expected to take care of his needs (this is especially difficult for the women who have to wait in long lines in order to get into the bathroom), and be back in his seat by the designated minute. After a break, there is always ten or fifteen minutes spent getting the medical-problem trainees into the back row, and the nonmedical trainees seated elsewhere.

After the break, the trainer reviews the "est chart of thought." This is a confusing table of mental processes that outlines the necessary steps to obtaining real experience in life by getting past all of the unneeded information that keeps people in a non-experiencing experiencing state. This non-experience experience is what prevents everyone from living. Many hours are spent describing this philosophy because, needless to say, most of the trainees don't understand it. Finally, the trainees begin to have a basic understanding of the Processes. Ironically, though, the next day, everyone is told that all the data that they had previously received on Saturday had been a lie.

The day passes on into evening, and the trainer continues to assault the concept of belief. As a result, the trainer is constantly peppered with questions. People are sharing misunderstandings, fear, anger, and rage over the data being provided. (Occasionally, someone is still turning in a candy bar.)

But from out of all of this, finally there is some message. It is that of responsibility. The trainee is told that he must experience responsibility. Up until now, his life had been a series of non-experiences. Punctuated with non-aliveness. A propensity to blame others for the pattern of his life. "When you are responsible, you get to experience that you didn't just happen to be standing in the middle of the highway when the light turned green. You put yourself there. And it is your responsibility to acknowledge that."

People spend their whole lives resisting responsibility. As a result, their lives don't work. They spend so much time resisting that they wind up going in the direction opposite to which they wish to travel. "It is much easier to ride the horse in the direction he's going," the trainer says. "Life works when you choose it, not when you resist it."

Only when you take responsibility for life and choose it can it work for you. Otherwise, life will be a rip-off. Constantly running you, constantly victimizing you.

This theme of responsibility is always strong enough to put at least six people to sleep. (And they are allowed to sleep on the est theory that, while sleeping, they aren't putting on an "act," and therefore some of the truth can get through.)

Finally, a dinner break is announced. The assistant comes forth and announces the locations of all the nearby restaurants. He also covers rides. This is nothing more than allowing people the opportunity to share rides home together, and sometimes sleeping quarters. (It is now the policy of est to make it clearly understood that the Organization holds no responsibility toward people who ride and live together during the training.) Ninety minutes are allowed for this break. People rush out of the room and head for the bathrooms and food. It is a strange sight to walk into a New York City restaurant, and see everyone identified with a name tag. However, it is an even stranger sight to see 250 people with name tags wandering through the hotel not speaking to one another. This occurs occasionally when the trainees are instructed not to speak with one another at a break due to the particular stage of the training.

The dinner break usually occurs about twelve hours into the training. By the time trainees get this food break, often they are not hungry. Or they eat solely because food is something familiar and nonthreatening.

After the dinner break, there is much sharing in the training room. est volunteers scurry up and down the aisles, presenting each sharing trainee with the microphone. Often there is a race between volunteers to see who can reach a trainee first. During this time, the "pain sharing" comes about. The room is alive with headaches, backaches, stomach pains, and leg cramps.

As a reward for the endless hours of badgering, the trainer begins the healing process. Trainees who have headaches, backaches, etc. are encouraged to concentrate on the pain. To visualize it. Look for its shape, size, color, texture. Choose to have it. And then watch it disappear. Miraculously, smiling trainees claim that their pains are gone. In choosing to have the headache, the trainee must also take responsibility for why he or she has it. (One trainee, suffering a weekly migraine during the first day of the training, "disappeared" her headache. But not until she experienced the fact that she was using that headache to avoid family responsibility at home. It was much easier to place the blame elsewhere. Another woman had a terrible backache. It disappeared when she experienced her mother hitting her on the back. As a young girl coming into womanhood, her mother had wanted her to have good posture so that she would be popular. Her backaches had emanated from not standing up straight.)

The highlight of the day comes at the very end. At this time, after the pains have been repaired, trainees are guided through their first real Process. Essentially, this is directed meditation and, in many ways, is quite similar to Transcendental Meditation, TM. Trainees are instructed to uncross their arms and legs and to relax. Under the direction of the trainer, the trainees put themselves into a restful state. From there, everyone imagines a beach. (This can be a favorite beach already in existence or a fantasized one.) The Process takes quite a long time (one to two hours) and during that period, trainees are constantly dropping off to sleep and, many times, going unconscious. The beach is created by the individual for his own personal use. Its purpose is to allow the person a restful respite from the pressures of the outside world. (These Processes are meant to be a part of the total experience of est. Therefore, the trainee, as a graduate, will continue to use the Processes and the beach as a form of meditation and inspiration in his everyday life.)

Generally speaking, trainees come out of the Processes feeling much more relaxed and at peace with themselves. Before ending the training for the night, everyone is shown how to go to sleep, how to set a mental alarm so that a mechanical one is not needed, and how to wake up refreshed in the morning. (When I went home that night at 2:00 A.M., I was exhausted but so keyed up I was unable to sleep. I put myself through the Process that would insure me sleep, a nonmechanical awakening, and mental refreshment upon arising. The next morning I did not wake up on my own. As a matter of fact, the alarm, which I had set as a backup, rang for twenty minutes before I heard it. And I felt sick and depressed when I woke up. But in all fairness to est, the Process was so effective at putting me to sleep that I was unable to complete it as instructed for the alarm clock and mental-refreshment portion.)

Before being dismissed from the training, everyone was informed that the second day of the training would involve a Truth Process . . . a means by which people could solve and rid themselves of major problems in their lives. A sure crowd-pleaser.

CHAPTER VII

The End of the First Weekend

In spite of the stern reminder from the previous evening to be seated by 9:30 A.M., there were a number of latecomers that first Sunday morning. They were all held up at the door until they had individually admitted to breaking an est agreement. To further enforce their wrongdoings, the trainer stopped in mid-sentence to point them out as they entered the room—here were perfect examples of people whose lives weren't working because they constantly broke agreements. Suitably chastened, they all sat down in the remaining seats.

One fascinating aspect of the est seating arrangements is the number of chairs. Chairs are always provided for the exact number of trainees. There is never an extra one in the room. If a trainee should drop out or leave for any reason, his chair is immediately removed.

The second day begins with sharing. Considering that the trainees have only about five hours of sleep under their belts, a tremendous amount had gone on in their heads. One mid-fifties man, who was seated in the medically exempt row for a back problem, spoke about what had gone on for him upon arising in the morning.

"I got up and did my exercises as I do each morning. Then I joined my wife for breakfast. I sat there looking at her and this great sadness came over me. Suddenly I realized why my back hurt so much for all these years. It was my guarantee that Emily would pay attention to me upon command. For the twenty-five years we have been married, I was never able to tell her how much I need her. And I didn't tell her this morning. But I hope before the training is over that I can."

A man in his forties stood up and shared his experience. "I came home last night and walked into my empty bedroom. My wife and I have been divorced for several years. A framed picture of me, taken about five years ago at my office, was on her old dresser. I looked at it very closely. And I saw that even five years ago, when I was in my thirties, the sadness in my life was showing right through that picture of me. Big as life. This morning, I looked at it again in the light of day, and I had to turn my head away." At this point, the man began to weep. "Then I thought about my two children. They're fifteen and seventeen years old. And I realized that for all these years I have been non-experiencing them. They're practically all grown up and ready to move away and lead lives of their own, and I've never really known them. Oh, God."

A number of the trainees began to cry and moan. A lot of what was being said reached everyone.

Another young man raised his hand to share. "I wanted to share what was going on with me. But after hearing these other stories, I feel as if mine isn't worth much. However, I'm going to talk anyway. For a long time, whenever I've gone to parties or been around girls, I've felt really uncomfortable. I "Got" that feeling uncomfortable is my thing. That's what I'm stuck in."

A chubby young woman talked about all the poor

relationships she was always having with men. No one really loved her. She was alone and miserable. "I try so hard, but no one ever stays with me for more than six months." The trainer strode up the aisle and planted himself directly in front of this woman. "No one ever stays with you because you're so busy running your goddamn 'act,' you don't even have time to notice that life is passing you by. You're a perfect example of an asshole, a fucking machine." The woman flinched and cowered at his words. Tears began to flow down her cheeks. On and on, he verbally beat her until she finally admitted that the reason she was so overweight was that food made her sleepy and she could go to bed without facing her life. (When the confrontation was over, it was as if a miraculous burden had been lifted from her shoulders. Her features smoothed out, and she actually looked quite pretty. Ironically, at the end of the dinner break that evening, she was the only one I saw eating a candy bar.)

After the sharing was completed, the trainer devoted a number of hours to lecture. Much of it repeated the concept of the "est chart of thought," which divides people's lives into experience and non-experience. Only today, there was a new twist: none of it was true. "Anything believed is a lie. Only experience is the truth," the trainees are told. Needless to say, this set a good majority of the trainees back a step or two. Confusion reigned. Question after question confirmed that no one seemed to understand what was happening. But the trainer said that was all okay. Everyone had to go through this state of confusion in order to be prepared for the Truth Process, which was coming up next. "Confusion is the first step toward 'natural knowing,'" he said. "And that's where you all eventually want to be." Natural knowing, according to est, is the pinnacle of living and experiencing.

Finally, the trainer moved to the subject of the Truth Process and exactly what it was. The trainees were all told to think of a problem or pattern that has been running their lives, and of which they would like to rid themselves. Hour after hour the trainer explains to everyone just how to pick a problem and how to phrase it in their minds. Most people got hung up in concepts. For example, "I want to stop feeling fat" is a concept. "I want to get over the anger associated with my mother for telling me I am fat" is a problem.

The trainer then demonstrated how the Truth Process works. A young male volunteer was found in the audience, willing to share his problem for the Process, so the other trainees could see how it works. His problem: "Anger and bitterness associated with his father who had lied and stolen from him."

Under the direction of the trainer, Bill then put himself into a meditative state, similar to the one trainees had all gone through at the end of the previous evening. By taking Bill through the early days of his life, when his mother and father were being divorced, he was able to determine why he felt that he was unworthy: because his father had divorced his mother and *left him* behind with no explanation other than the fact that he was too young to understand. Bill understood that he was no good, otherwise his father would not have left. And it affected his entire life for the next thirty years. As a result, Bill constantly set himself up so that his father took advantage of him, stole from him, got him fired from a job, embarrassed him. Always it was his father's fault. It wasn't until well into the Process that Bill finally experienced that he was allowing himself to be victimized by his father so that he wouldn't have to take responsibility for himself. Bill broke down and cried, as did many in the audience. On that sober note, the Truth Process began for everyone.

"Remove the chairs to the back of the room. Find a space on the floor. Uncross your arms and legs. Close your eyes. Go into your space and start to relax." The trainer takes the trainees through the standard process, up to the point before they "go to the beach." They are instructed to repeat their problem to themselves. Taking everyone through specific situations, the trainer skilfully manages to reach to the inner emotional depths of practically everyone present. Several people begin to cry as the Process goes on. Several more start to moan. A man screams.

"The room is going to get very noisy. Keep your eyes closed. If your problem disappears, or partially disappears, roll over and go to the beach." More people join the screaming and the crying. The rustle of vomit bags is heard as they are passed among the sick. As the Process continues, more people begin to get sick. After what seems an endless period of time to most people—about an hour—the room begins to quiet. The screams fade to moans. The wailing and crying become soft weeping and moaning. The trainer directs everyone to his or her beach in order to complete the Process. The trainees relax and are finally brought out of their semitrance state. Most everyone looks dazed and weary.

It's 9:00 in the evening and a dinner break is announced. People pick themselves up and wander out of the room. (During my training, we all meandered around a girl who was lying unconscious on the floor as a result of the Process.)

Dinner seems to find most trainees with diminished appetites and their "acts" quickly back in order, although not in the same perfected manner. Dinner is eaten in a fairly relaxed manner since no one has any idea of what is in store for them after this ninety-minute break.

Upon arriving back from the dinner break, the trainees find the chairs have been rearranged in six long rows, extending ominously across the room. Everyone is directed to sit down and fill the rows from the center out, as they always do. The trainees are told they are going to go through a Process to be with people. To the uninitiated, that seems a simple task. Any grad knows that it's Danger. The next item on the est agenda is what's commonly known on the street as The Danger Process.

The trainer explains that each row of people in turn will file up onto the platform at the front of the room. All they need do is stand there and "be with someone" in the room. That is, put your arms at your side, stand up straight and find someone in the audience with whom you can make eye contact.

The first row is told to go to the platform and make eye contact. Watching this Process is somewhat like being transmitted to a combination insane asylum/torture ward. What happens to the trainees is absolutely incredible. The trainees at the front of the room look out into the sea of faces and begin to smile. The trainer starts screaming, "Cut your 'act.' Quit smiling. It's costing you your life." Most of the smiles quickly vanish. A few diehards start to laugh. The trainer and other est staff march up to these people. The trainer screams. est staff do nothing but stand in front of a trainee and look him directly in the eyes. Women start to cry. Men clench their fists and tense up. The staring continues on the part of est staff. The trainer is yelling, "Let it all come up. Cut your 'act' and see what you've been doing to your life. You'd rather be right than alive. You're all goddamned fucking machines. Complete assholes. Nothing in your life works for you and you wonder why.

Look what you are doing to yourselves. Standing up here smiling, for Christ's sake. What's so goddamn funny? The fact that you're pissing your life away?"

Like a scene from a horror movie, people began to fall apart right before your eyes. The man who had never been able to tell his wife that he really needed her went into a catatonic state. The woman who confessed to never having an orgasm cried until she collapsed. A young man, who had come with his married sister, cried hysterically. A tall, thin man swayed like a willow in the wind. Finally, he fainted on the floor. The trainer ran over and started screaming at him. "Cut the act, Michael. That's just a big fucking game you're playing. Get up, Michael, and be with someone for the first time in your life. You're so dead, you can't even be with anyone. Get up, Michael." And, miraculously, Michael gets up, looks out into the audience, and connects with someone until he repeats the Process. He winds up in a heap in the corner, like a discarded bundle of rags.

After about fifteen minutes of this, the row of people is finally released and they are allowed to go back to their seats. They are instructed to make contact with other trainees who are about to take that walk to Danger.

The Process is repeated. Row after row of trainees go to the front of the room to "be with someone." Always, in each row, there is crying, screaming, fainting, vomiting.

In order to get the full impact of what happens during the Danger Process, I would like to explain what happened in my training.

Upon arriving back from dinner, confident that my life had been turned around and it was all cake from here on in (my Truth Process had been extremely helpful in clearing up a situation that had been running my life for the last nineteen years), I was surprised to see the room looking so austere, with its long rows of perfectly aligned chairs and the small platform at the front of the room.

We were told that the next Process was designed to get us in touch with our feelings and to acquaint ourselves with "being with someone without our 'acts.'" We were told that most people can better describe someone else's shoes than they can the same person's face. I was seated in the second row. The first row premiered on the platform, lining themselves up against a strip of tape that had been placed the length of the platform. Three-foot intervals marked where each person was to stand.

The Process began. I looked at a number of people on the platform who were facing me. No one returned my watchful eyes. As a matter of fact, such a long time went by before I finally made eye contact with a young woman standing on the platform that I had begun to think people didn't like me. Why wouldn't anyone look at me? I'm a nice-looking, kind sort of person. Feeling more confident that I was liked after all, I was shocked when the woman began to cry. Softly at first, then with a more hysterical tone. Her fists clenched into tight balls. And her arms moved away from her sides.

From out of nowhere, a small brigade of est staff marched down a side aisle and across the front of the platform. Strategically they positioned themselves in front of trainees. The woman with whom I had contact was cut off by an est staff member. Although I could no longer see her, I could hear her moaning and screaming.

Once again I scanned the row, but no one would make eye contact with me. So instead, I began to watch the people. A long-haired young man began to cry—hysterically. Snot dripped out of his nose and into his beard. His mouth hung open and a long string of spit dribbled out onto his flannel shirt. Two people fainted and one person threw up. Every time an est staff member removed himself from in front of a trainee, that person was usually dissolved into mush.

"Holy shit," I thought. "I can't believe what's happening to these people. I was really beginning to get nervous because my row was next. I've done a lot of public speaking and am used to facing large crowds of people. Our trainer had told us this would be nothing, nor would it do us any good, during the Process. I thought about the friend who had been most instrumental in my going through est. "You motherfucker. I don't need this shit. You goddamn son-of-a-bitching motherfucker. How could you send me to the slaughter this way?"

After what seemed like an eternity, the trainer dismissed the first row. I was really beginning to sweat. My palms were clammy. I didn't know if I could handle what was coming up next. Then the trainer announced that Row Three should come up on the platform. Row Three! My row had been passed over. God, I was psyched out. So I sat there and watched the same thing happen all over again. What transformation takes place up there? My pea brain just couldn't begin to comprehend it. I had studied a little bit of this in Psych 201 in college, but to witness it is something else again. And to know that I was going to go through it was enough to blow my mind away. Another row was called—not mine. Again, I watched them perform.

It was interesting though. By the time the third row of trainees had finished, I could actually predict who was going to freak out *before they actually did so*. Not that I'm a psychic by any means. est staff know, too. This is evidenced by the fact that there is always a backup team standing behind the platform, waiting to catch people or support them as they fall. Not so coincidentally, they are always standing behind the people who go to pieces.

Finally, Row Two is called. The waiting is over. As I step up onto the platform, I think, "Paul, you motherfucker. You lousy little motherfucker. I'll kill you for this."

I find my slot on the tape and start to make eye contact with someone in the audience. Once again, I am plagued with the same problem. No one wants to look at me. "Is there something especially wrong with me that people are constantly looking away?" Strangely enough, it wasn't nearly so bad as I had expected standing up there. I was fairly relaxed, although I must admit that my legs were shaking a little, and my knees felt watery. Hoorah. Someone finally looked at me for a few minutes before looking away.

Again, I looked out into the sea of faces. The guy with the snot hanging out of his nose was still crying hysterically. And then a staff member arrived and positioned herself about three inches from the tip of my nose. "Here it goes," I thought. "I am going to be an embarrassed mess by the time she walks away from me." In a way, though, I was really glad to have someone looking at me, someone whom I could be assured wouldn't look away. And instead of crying, fainting or getting catatonic, I began to feel nice inside. It was good to look at another person, and know that you didn't have to make conversation or be amusing, witty or intelligent. When she departed, I was sad to see her go. After what seemed like an eternity, our row was sent back into the audience.

When the Danger Process was completed, we were once again directed to remove our chairs to the back of the room and find a place to lie down on the floor.

God, I was getting tired. First the Truth Process. Then the Danger Process. Now what would they possibly do to us?

On the floor, in a "meditative state," we were directed to keep our eyes closed and to pretend that we were either an actor or actress. Once again, the trainer warned us that the room would become very noisy. We were then directed to become very afraid of the person lying next to us. The person lying next to me was a very attractive woman, and I really couldn't get into being afraid of her. But then I remembered the guy lying next to her. He had thrown up during the Danger Process. I thought about how I would feel if he threw up on me and I became very afraid. Then we were directed to become afraid of the people surrounding us. I couldn't get worked up for this Process but, apparently, plenty of other people could. The screams started coming. By the time the trainer had everyone frightened of the entire universe, the room was alive with screaming. Once again, I could hear people retching all about me. For a fleeting moment I opened my eyes and looked out onto mass hysteria. That was enough to bring me back. After everyone had been ordered to imagine that he or she was afraid of everyone else in the universe, the trainer told each of us to imagine that we were the most frightening people in the world. That everyone else was scared to death of us.

The final order, before releasing us for the night, was to spend the rest of the week scaring people with our inner ability to do so. It was 2:15 in the morning. Bone tired, I dragged myself to a cab and rode back to my West Side apartment. What are they going to do to us next week? I wondered.

CHAPTER VIII

The Mid-Week Training

The Mid-Week Training takes place at a hotel similar to the ones in which the other training sessions have occurred. It is attended by the same 250 people who had been in training together the previous weekend. Although it is not a required part of the training, the great majority of trainees attend this three-and-one-half-hour session.

The Mid-Week Training is very much like a revival meeting. Acquaintances are reunited like long-lost friends, and even the shyest, most retired people speak with other est trainees and share some of their experiences in casual conversation.

The Mid-Week Training is very much like a continuation of the training from the previous weekend except that there is much more emphasis on the sharing of experiences. In a way, the Mid-Week Training could be called more aptly a "Survival Meeting." The trainees, after the first weekend, tend to be either incredibly high or incredibly low as a result of the training. There doesn't seem to be much of an in-between status. Therefore, as a result of the sharing, the trainees become more secure about what they are feeling. For example, a man who was very depressed as a result of the experiences from the previous weekend was told that he should stay with that feeling, that that was what he "Got" from the training. That kind of comment is indigenous to all of the Mid-Week Training Seminars. As a matter of fact, it is not unfair to say that, once you've been to one Mid-Week Training Seminar, you've practically been to them all. There are few differences in what goes on.

There is always one especially interesting aspect of the Mid-Week Training and that deals with the relationships that have been repaired as a result of the est training. In listening to the sharing, it would be easy to get the idea that no one in the world is speaking with his or her parents, sisters or brothers! Literally, dozens of people in any given Mid-Week Training will stand up and share that they have spoken with a mother, father, cousin, ex-best friend, for the first time in years. And by the reactions of the people in the audience, you could easily see that there were dozens of other people who had felt the same way about wanting to get in touch with a parent or other close person and hadn't done it.

The sharing is a very important aspect of the est training. Not only does it enable the trainees to bring their feelings out into the open and share them publicly, without an "act," but in addition it aids the other trainees as well. It is often stated by est and many of the other disciplines that people's lives are run by the same three or four problems. And those problems are probably the only thing about est that aren't individual experiences. For example, a trainee may share that he hates his father. A woman might recognize the great fear she has of dying. A husband may realize that he hates his wife. And a woman may realize that she eats as a means of covering up her loneliness. Naturally, these are all very real items for the people who are sharing them. But they are also, in many cases, very real items for the trainees who are listening to them. The scenes of dying, loneliness, and hate are commonplace. As a result, there is often fierce identification among all of the trainees. During the sharing, a nonparticipating trainee may be able to get in touch with a very real problem as a result of what someone else shared.

For example, one woman told how, as a little girl of eight or nine, she had watched her grandmother, who lived with her and her family, slowly and painfully die of cancer. Back in those days, patients did not go to the hospital, so the grandmother died in bed at home. As a result, the little girl became so obsessed with sickness and death that she could no longer take the responsibility for it. When a friend would have an illness, she would disappear until the friend got better. Visiting people at home was too much for her.

Another woman, sitting in the audience and listening to the story that the woman told, suddenly realized that she, too, was obsessed with sickness and dying. Cancer seemed to run in her family. Her brother, mother, two uncles and four cousins had all died from it at rather early ages. She was aware that she was very frightened of cancer and of dying. But what she got in touch with as a result of listening to the woman was the fact that, although she was frightened of dying, death was what she was actually choosing. She was accomplishing this by not taking proper medical care of herself, avoiding doctors, ignoring checkup notices, etc. She was frightened to die, yet she chose death as a means of getting out of the situation. It was easier to die and get it over with than it was to actually live and have death lurking in the background.

Another simpler example of this is the man who shared that he called his father for the first time in fourteen years and communicated with him. He had been scared about making the call for a number of reasons. He had toyed with it over the last couple of years but, somehow, it was always easier to be "right" than to be alive and have the relationship with his father. But, as a result of the training, he did call his father, patched up the relationship, and made plans to visit with him.

As a result, a woman who was in the audience and had much the same experience decided that she would call her father. She, too, had been putting off the confrontation for several years because of the fact that she envisioned the conversation as being extremely painful and bitter. After listening to the man's story and hearing about his telephone conversation, she chose to believe that the call to her father would give her more value than it would pain. She called him and they were reunited. As a result, she was able to complete her relationship with her father and that helped her immensely in her everyday life.

Not everyone has such remarkable experiences as a result of the training. Many trainees attend the Mid-Week Training in a terrifically depressed state. Very often, this is as a result of an "emotional, surgical procedure." Many people, while under emotional stress, often refer to the fact that they feel as if they had been in surgery and have been cut open, but nothing has been removed and the individual has not yet been sewn up again. Since the "operation" is incomplete, this often leads to a feeling of vulnerability, depression, anxiety, etc.

One man shared with the audience that he had come out of the est training on Sunday really feeling terrific. He had gone to his job on Monday morning ready to make tremendous transformations and to really take responsibility for what he was doing, something that he hadn't been doing in the past. He walked in on

Monday morning, was called into his boss' office, and fired. Just when life seemed to be beginning for him, he found it was ending. (That kind of statement is quickly recognized as a "dump" on the part of the trainee. The trainer is often quick to point out that the trainee is unwilling to take responsibility for his life.)

Many of the trainees get depressed during the first weekend and they never shake it until they come back to the est training on the following weekend. Therefore, the Mid-Week Training finds them in a most unhappy state. Those trainees who have a "continuous depression" are often the people with the greatest amount of resistance. They are also the ones who know they are going to have to give up the resistance if they are going to be alive and take responsibility in their everyday living situations. At the time, they may not be consciously aware of the phase through which they are passing but, most often, the depression passes in the second weekend and these people have a real sense of "Getting It."

A lot of time is spent in the Mid-Week Training discussing the Processes that were learned in the first weekend. One of the Processes that especially intrigues the trainees is the one in which they are able to set a mental alarm clock and wake up feeling refreshed, even on just a few hours' sleep. Throughout the room, trainees shared stories of how they woke up before they would normally wake up, feeling refreshed and alive; that they got to the office on time after being habitually late for years. They were happy and talkative and full of energy. As a result of this Process, alarms and clock radios were being cast aside like so much dirty laundry! Other people found the Processes extremely useful in getting to sleep. And one amazing benefit to all of the pain sufferers was that during the week, few people had headaches, backaches, and the normal aches and pains that went with their everyday lives.

One of the tenets that pervades the est training is the scene that people's lives don't work because they don't keep their agreements. So, during the Mid-Week Training, one of the items of sharing was the "concessions" of trainees who had broken agreements since the training ended three days ago. For example, a woman drank a glass of wine before she remembered that she had agreed not to, and a young man confessed that he had snorted coke on Monday night and it had blown his mind away. Several people took aspirin as a result of severe headaches and one man got drunk. However, the difference at the Mid-Week Training was that the trainees were not severely reprimanded about their broken agreements. The very fact that they had shared them was proof that they took the responsibility for them. The other very big difference that occurs at the Mid-Week Training Seminar is the difference in attitude on the part of the trainees with reference to questioning what is going on. The Pre-Training Seminar was filled with questions by anxious trainees as to why they couldn't go to the bathroom, smoke, eat, talk, move, etc. Although these questions were always answered with such profound statements as "because it works," there is a terrific lessening of this need to know why. At the Pre-Training Seminar, 95 percent of the audience participation is made up with questions to the trainer.

Although many profound and startling differences occurred in the trainees over a very short period of time, there was much more an acceptance of these differences as "what is." In the Mid-Week Training, the trainees devote about 95 percent of their time to sharing, and about five percent to questions.

Another big difference in the Mid-Week Training is the lessening need for sympathy on the part of the trainees. During the first weekend, when trainees shared situations that were troubling them or that they were experiencing, there was a lot of "dumping" going on. The trainer, of course, was always quick to react to this, and many times during the second day, the audience would visibly shudder when they would hear another "act." The trainees seemed to be much more *without* their defenses at the Mid-Week Training. The sharing, as a result, is much more truthful and experiential in nature. When you think about the implications of these transformations that take place in such a short period of time, it is really quite remarkable. For example, the man who had not spoken with his father in years chose to call him on the telephone as a result of approximately thirty hours of being with himself in intensive training. The woman who had been dying got unstuck from it and for the first time since she was a little girl was able to start living. That is some pretty heavy stuff to handle.

When the sharing is completed, the trainees are directed in a Process whereby they can expand the spaces of their mind. This starts off in the usual way of relaxing the feet and legs and body, arms, shoulders, and head. The trainees are then directed to bring into their lives people surrounding them, the people in their homes, in their offices, in their cities and states, etc. The purpose of this particular Process is to show the trainees just how much space they can provide for themselves, people they love, and the world in general. After the Process is completed, the trainees are dismissed for the evening.

Generally speaking, the trainees often leave the Mid-Week Training Seminar disappointed in what went on. They had all been told that the Mid-Week Training experience is a very valuable experience. However, it could probably be concluded that the first weekend is so dramatic and earth shattering for most of the trainees, that a three-and-one-half-hour seminar can't really hold a candle to it.

CHAPTER IX

The Second Saturday

The second weekend begins with high hopes for all of the trainees. For many of them, one week has made the difference in their lives. There is always much excitement about sharing all that happened during the week with the trainer. This is always the first shock to the trainees when they discover that the man whom they had hated and then come to love from the previous weekend is no longer with them.

Instead, there appears on the horizon another Werner lookalike, this time a little bit taller and a little bit thinner, and a little bit gentler in manner. (It seems that the way est runs the show is that the trainer for the first weekend is a very strong, militarylike version of Werner and for the second weekend, they provide a trainer who is a man of gentler nature and who deals on a much more friendly level with the trainees.)

The trainer begins the day by reviewing est and its basic tenets. That is, again there was a detailed discussion of the need to take responsibility in an individual's life, the right to choose, the need to come from cause and not effect, and the right to accept yourself exactly the way you are. That means even if you aren't perfect, you're okay. The trainer also devoted time to discussing experience—that which enables every trainee and est graduate to live a life based in reality. In other words, the only Truth is experience. If someone tells you something and you believe it, then it's a lie.

During the prior week, that had caused a great deal of confusion among the trainees. This week, hearing the same thing, most of the people reacted with a great deal of enthusiasm and excitement. There is almost a ripple running through the crowd of people anxious to share their experiences.

Before the trainer moves on to the sharing portion of the day, he tells the trainees that this is the really important weekend. For whatever they had gotten from est prior to this second Saturday, it was only equivalent to about fifteen percent of the training. The balance, or 85 percent, was going to be attained over the next two-day period. That caused even more excitement. You could sense that the trainees had had some incredible experiences during the week, and the thought that the major value from the training was still to come almost seemed to be too much to bear.

The new trainer, although still a Werner lookalike, is less estian in nature. He doesn't use nearly so much of the est language and lingo. And his voice is much softer in tone. He doesn't have anywhere near the military bearing that the first trainer had. This is not coincidental; it is scheduled to be like this. Werner has it all planned.

It's very interesting the second weekend to see all of the trainees dragging their extra sweaters and jackets and pillows to the training to keep them warmer and more comfortable during the endless hours of sitting on hard, straight-backed chairs that are provided. Except the second weekend, the rooms in which the trainees sit are kept extremely warm. As a result, the trainees started shedding all the layers of clothes that they had worn to the session. As a result of the heat in the rooms, the trainees kept dropping off to sleep. You could see that the heat was practically suffocating many of them. As soon as they would begin to doze, the trainer would yell at them to wake up. This was in direct contrast to what had gone on the prior weekend when it was okay to sleep. (As a matter of fact, the trainees are told at the Pre-Training that they can sleep through the entire est training and still "Get It.")

The sharing that goes on the second weekend of est is always somewhat like an evangelical revival meeting! Miracles were shared by the dozens. One woman, who claimed she never had an orgasm, had her first one with her husband during the week. Several trainees announced that they had received large raises. Another got a promotion as a result of a confrontation with his boss. At least a half-dozen people announced that they had spoken with one or more members of their family for the first time in years. Furthermore, it seemed that hardly anyone needed to own an alarm clock anymore. The magical process that had been described during the prior weekend whereby people could wake up naturally and feel refreshed seemed to be working for dozens of the est trainees.

When the miracles were over, then the depressers began to speak up. It seems that not everyone gets a $10,000 raise and a reunion with his or her mother for their $250 fee. One man said he had seriously considered committing suicide during the week because he suddenly realized that his life was 75 percent completed and he had accomplished nothing. And est had really made him realize that he hadn't done a single thing. He didn't see how he could justify going on under those circumstances. Another man realized how

far away he was from his wife. After twenty-five years
of marriage, they actually had very little in common. It
was a very sad awakening for him and he felt that he
would really rather have not had it. Certainly, after
twenty-five years, he couldn't just walk out on his wife.
Plus the fact he would have no idea what he would do
if he were to leave her. A woman stood up to share the
fact that she recognized, after last week's training, that
her marriage was a mess. She said she tried all week to
talk with her husband about it and to try and come to
some sort of conclusion or understanding.

It seemed as if the trainer was just waiting for this
woman to stand up and make this announcement. He
looked at her name tag, called her by name, and asked
her to come up on the stage. Then he took a great big
heavy dictionary (to which the trainers constantly
refer) and dropped it on the floor. It landed with a
heavy thud. "Now try and pick up that dictionary," he
said. The woman stooped down and picked it up. The
trainer took the dictionary from her and dropped it
back on the floor. "I said, 'try and pick up the dictionary.'" Again, the woman stooped down and picked up
the dictionary. He took it away from her again and
repeated the process several more times. By the fifth
time, the woman still had not "Gotten" that you can't *try*
to pick up the dictionary. Either you pick it up, or you
don't pick it up. "You can't *try* to pick up that dictionary. You either pick it up or you don't pick it up. Now
you've picked it up five times. Never once did you *try*
to pick it up. Now you have the nerve to stand up and
tell everybody here in this audience that you *tried* all
week to fix your marriage? That's ridiculous."

That demonstration is the signal for the trainer
to launch into the day's lecture, a long and tedious dis-
sertation that bores most of the audience into sleep. The
lecture is very technical in nature, dealing with objec-

tive reality and knowledge. Hours are spent describing reality and its relationship to experience and society. It is finally determined, after grueling hours and much dozing off by the trainees, that the only reality that exists is that reality that is there by agreement. Everything else is an illusion. This is much the same concept as the idea that anything experienced is truth, anything believed is a lie.

It is very heavy material, and it takes its toll on the trainees. You can sense the amount of effort that is going into understanding what the trainer is talking about. Yet, when the first break comes and the trainees get to talk with one another, it is quickly determined that hardly anyone knows what the trainer has just addressed himself to for the last four or five hours.

After the first break, there is a discussion on the part of the trainer as to how many people broke est agreements during the week. He asked for anyone who had broken an agreement to stand up. About fifty percent of the room will stand up as a result of that question. Then he asked the second *big* question. How many people think they *might* have broken an agreement during the week? Another large group of people stood up and joined the others who were already standing. It now seems that about two-thirds of the room is standing up as a result of the broken-agreement question. "Good," the trainer says. "For your information, if any of you *think* you have broken an agreement, you have broken an agreement." While everyone is still standing, shuffling their weight from foot to foot, the trainer points out that this is a perfect example of why everyone's life is not working for him or her. "Just look at the number of people standing. About 75 percent of you couldn't keep an agreement. And you wonder why your life always gets fucked up. You're just machines. You've got to learn that keeping agreements is the start of keeping a better life."

After the trainer finishes demonstrating how people muck up their lives, he goes back to the lecture that he had been previously delivering and that no one understood. From reality and illusion, he launches into a discussion of survival as it relates to the mind. This is an extremely important part of the training and, unfortunately, is generally lost on a good number of the trainees who have already "gone unconscious." The mind works on a need or survival basis. Everything the mind does is based on this specific emphasis. And the mind survives by calling up past experiences and utilizing them in everyday situations. As a result, people wind up having their lives run by past experiences and never know why. The trainer gives the following example. A little boy is peddling on his tricycle up and down the driveway. His mother has sternly lectured him that he is not allowed to go out in the street. He could get killed. After peddling up and down the driveway for quite some time, little Johnnie decides that it is not enough. He has to go out and explore other areas. So he peddles down the driveway and out into the street. He peddles along for just a little way when a car comes speeding up from behind him. The driver steps on the brakes, honks the horn, and comes to a screeching halt before he hits little Johnnie. Johnnie, as a result, falls off his tricycle and cuts his forehead open on the curb. His mother runs out of the house, yelling and screaming, and rushes Johnnie off to the doctor where he gets several stitches in his head.

A number of years later, Johnnie is walking down the street in the Village and is passing a bicycle shop. Just as he gets past the window, a car comes to a screeching halt in the street and the driver angrily honks his horn at a jaywalker. Johnnie faints on the sidewalk.

Johnnie blacked out as a means of survival. And that's a perfect example of what so often happens to people in their present lives. Their minds react from *past* experience and, most often, that experience is no longer appropriate to the situation. By blacking out and not coping with what was happening, the mind was enabling itself to survive.

Unfortunately, this happens all too often in everyone's life. They falsely react to situations as a way of surviving.

The trainer then divides the mind into three levels of pain:

Pain Level No. 1
Pain Level No. 2
Pain Level No. 3

Pain Level Nos. 1 and 3 deal with the mind's ability to survive, while Pain Level No. 2, much less important, deals in physical pain. The Pain Level No. 1 has to have a pain, a loss of consciousness or awareness, and a threat to survival. Pain Level No. 3 is the mind's reaction to Pain Level No. 1. During Pain Level No. 3, the mind will do whatever it can to avoid what it considers a potential Pain Level No. 1. What is even more threatening is that many times the individual does not even consciously recall what the Pain Level No. 1 experience was.

What happens as a result is that people are never reacting to what they *think* they are reacting to. Based on this kind of a pattern, it becomes fairly simple to perceive why most people have so much difficulty communicating with one another. It isn't until an individual can work back to the original Pain Level No. 1 that he can clear up the problem.

For example, one woman shared the fact that she always felt terrible in the morning; she was unable to accomplish anything until after 10:00 A.M.; she never wanted to speak with anyone until after 10:00 A.M. When the trainer asked her how long she had been feeling this way, it stopped her dead in her tracks. She was thirty-one years old and she had to think all the way back until she was five years of age before she could remember feeling good in the morning. It turned out that she used to get up each morning and go downstairs with her father before anyone else was out of bed, and watch him shave and talk with him. That was their private time together. During that time, the girl's mother and father began to have marital difficulties. The father took a lover and began to drink too much. Then followed open hostility between the mother and father.

As a little girl, she was very close to her mother. Her mother resented the fact that she shared this private time with her father. Although her mother never said anything directly to her, the little girl sensed she was doing something wrong. As she began to pull away from her father, he became angry with her for her disloyalty to him.

Pretty soon, it became an unpleasant thing for the little girl to get up in the morning. And as the years passed and the situation became worse and worse between her parents, it became more difficult for her to get up. Eventually, they divorced. But the feeling of sickness never disappeared. For nineteen years, the little girl, then grown into a woman, was feeling terrible when she got up in the morning. And it wasn't until she traced it back to a Pain Level No. 1 experience that she was finally able to "disappear" it.

This is a perfect example of a past situation running the person's life in the form of a Pain Level No. 3 experience. By avoiding everyone in the morning, and never feeling well enough to speak with anyone until after 10:00 A.M., the woman could get past the unpleasant hours and, therefore, "survive."

When people trace back their Pain Level No. 3 experiences until they finally come onto the Pain Level No. 1 experience, it can be a cognizant experience. A confrontation with a Pain Level No. 1 experience can diminish it considerably.

Of course, there is really nothing new about this concept of pain-level experiences. Freud dealt with it, Scientology deals with it, and est uses it too. However, the big difference between est and other disciplines or theories of the pain-level experiences is that in est you actually *experience* the Pain Level No. 1. The Truth Process, mentioned in an earlier chapter, is a perfect example of dealing with the Pain Level No. 1 experience, the considerations, the attitudes, the feelings, the emotions, and the images of what happened during a Pain Level No. 1 experience. It is an extremely painful thing to run through, but it does much to dissolve, or reduce, the pain-level experiences.

Dinner on that second Saturday night is a relatively calm affair. When the trainees arrive back from supper, they each find a plastic bag under their chair. The bags contain a fresh daisy, a real strawberry, a section of lemon, a smooth stone, a small cube of wood, and a small cube of metal. This is to be part of a Process in which the trainees experience all of the items that are in the bag. The Process that the trainees go through to experience these items is fun and amusing. It is one of the lighter moments of the est training.

First the trainees are directed to hold the lemon section up toward the light and bend the peel back. Most everyone is always amazed to see the streams of oil shoot up off the skin of the lemon. Combined with this is a lovely fragrance of fresh lemon. Next, the trainees are directed to study very carefully the outside of the strawberry. To notice all of the little tiny seeds, the color, and the texture. Next, they remove the green stem at the top and look down into the little hole. They stick their tongues in and taste it. Next, they get to eat the strawberry. There is always much laughter and kidding at this point. It is the first time that any food is allowed into the training room. The trainees all seem to think that if they had gone through this Process before dinner, everyone would have gobbled down the strawberry and lemon section before they could have ever "Gotten" a true experience of them! The square cube of wood and metal are used to demonstrate the different textures and smells of wood and metal. After the strawberry encounter, the trainer goes back to his lecture.

The evening ends with the trainer taking all of the trainees through a long (several hours') Process where they travel across the universe. Having traveled such a great distance, the trainees are finally released for the night. They are instructed to be back at the hotel, in their seats, by 9:30 A.M. the following day.

CHAPTER X

Graduation

The second Sunday is when everything happens. According to the trainer, eighty percent of the training comes on that final Sunday. And that's the day that everyone graduates, too.

The trainer starts off in a beautiful and excited mood. Today is going to be the day he shares the secret of life. Everyone can hardly wait.

Before he shares that secret, the trainer instructs the trainees on how to build a center, a safe place to go within each of the trainees, so that he or she can deal with all that has been experienced and that will be experienced in the future.

The trainees are then directed into a Process where they are in a meditative state. They are given instructions as to exactly how to build this center within themselves. Basically, it is a room, structure, or house, which contains everything the trainee would need to survive and to live happily. That means the trainee would have his favorite books and records, and other inanimate objects. In his imagination, the trainee starts with the foundation and literally, while sitting on the floor, builds this structure with his hands. The purpose behind this is to get a real sense of having created the center. The trainer guides the trainees in terms of the center so that it contains some very specific items. Among them is a special television screen and most important, a door, which the trainee operates, which allows people in and out of the center. This center is the equivalent of the training room; *i.e.*, it is a safe place. The trainee can always go there in his imagination and work out situations with which he is having difficulty dealing. In addition, he can bring other people down into his center and talk with them without having fear of being reprimanded or that the information will be held against him. By doing this imaginary exercise, the trainee is often able to confront Pain Level No. 3 and Pain Level No. 1 situations. Of course, whenever this happens, the trainee has added considerably to his ability to clear up life situations with which he has not otherwise been able to deal properly.

When the center is completed, the next stage of the Process is to invite an individual with whom the trainee wishes to straighten something out into it. All of this is an exercise to show the trainee how the center works and how he can use it after he is out of the est training program. You can begin to understand that an est graduate having been through this experience has a difficult time communicating just what it is all about to a nonestian.

When the center is built, the trainer returns to his lecture. The theme revolved around enlightenment. Ironically though, the trainer's definition of enlightenment is very unlike that of the dictionary, which says that enlightenment is the act of being endowed with truth or spiritual understanding. According to the trainer, enlightenment is nothing more than realizing that you are a machine. For hours the trainer delivers this lecture.

Somewhere along the line, the sense of excitement, which was so prevalent among the trainees at the beginning of the day, begins to turn to nervousness, anticipation and stress. They recognize that time is running out on the clock, even though they have no timepieces in the room, and still no one seems to "Get It." Finally, the trainer begins to yell at the trainees telling them that they are nothing more than machines and have to accept it and that's "Getting It." The trainees sit there in a dazed manner.

"That's it, you're machines. Nothing but machines and you've got to accept it. Come from a position of being a machine. You'll work from cause, not effect."

The trainees, of course, always wait for the trainer, at this point, to tell them it is a joke—to provide them with the real definition of "Getting It." But he doesn't. The fact that everyone is a machine is what the trainees have paid their $250 for.

Immediately, hands begin to wave frantically in the air. Everyone is protesting that they don't "Get It." Trainees all around the room claim that they don't "Get It." And with each claim, the trainer always responds that there is nothing to "Get." That that's it.

In one of the training sessions, when a young woman was told that "Getting It" was accepting the fact that she was a machine, she broke down and began to cry bitterly. She couldn't believe and she couldn't accept that "Getting It" was nothing at all. Not only did she feel that she had been ripped off, but if there is absolutely nothing to "Get" out of life except the fact that you are a machine, she couldn't see the sense of living. She stood there and cried and cried and cried and never once did the trainer offer to assist her in any way, other than to let the awful truth sink through. According to the trainer, you have no choice in life. This threw the crowd into an uproar, because it was contrary to everything they had been taught for three and one-half days. That was it, all 250 trainees were nothing more than a machine.

In spite of everything the trainer said, the trainees refused to believe that what they had been told was "It." What reinforced us even more was the fact that there was still time left in the evening. The trainees figured that the trainer was playing a joke on them and would shortly reverse everything he had said. As he continued to reinforce his theory, it simply blew everyone's mind.

And what the trainees had to say was true. There was more time left and there was more time to learn. However, the concept of being a machine created a real tension in the room. The trainees are very aware that there are not too many hours left in this day and if they are going to "Get" the meaning of life and be transformed, they are going to have to do it pretty quickly.

Finally, after the trainer has worked his way around the room and has listened to everyone's comments about "Getting It" and has reassured each of them as they say that they haven't "Got It" that they indeed did "Get It," he enters into the second phase of the lecture on "Getting It." " 'Getting It' is truly 'Getting' whatever you 'Get,' " he said. "If you are willing to accept your mind as it is and take responsibility for having created all of the situations in which you presently are and in which you always have been, then, in essence, you have chosen to do everything that has ever happened to you. At that point, you are in control of your life and you can 'Get' whatever you want." By this time, the trainees are so desperate to have something tangible to hold onto that even this meager new explanation of "Getting It" is acceptable to them. The trainer tells them that by taking responsibility for themselves and for what they have created, they then have the ability to move past enlightenment. That means they are no longer assholes or machines. Instead, they are perfect human beings. Needless to say, there were plenty of trainees who, at the time, didn't think this revelation was worth $250.

But the evening goes on. Shortly thereafter, a dinner break is announced, and groups of people rush out to discuss this new "Getting It" thing that they've just been told and to determine whether or not they have really been duped.

After dinner, the trainees returned to a sales pitch on the Graduate Seminar program, which only as a graduate of est could they attend. There were a number of lectures on subjects such as "What's so," "About sex," "Be here now," etc. Trainees were being offered this lecture series at a very minimal price and were encouraged to sign up immediately for it. Naturally, in all the est efficiency, there are pencils and application cards conveniently provided under each trainee's seat. When the Graduate Seminar sell is completed, the trainer goes back to his discussion of "Getting It." There are some more questions but, basically, most of the trainees have either accepted that they "Get It" or they are rather depressed about what they feel they have "Gotten." This is typical of what happens to the trainees at this point in the training.

On this last Sunday evening, after the trainees have "Gotten It," they graduate. Other est graduates are allowed to attend the graduation if they so desire. When the grads are finally allowed into the training room, they greet the trainees with a tremendous round of applause. Then, trainees and grads alike sit through another lecture about making life work. There is a personality profile in which all of the trainees participate, and then there is graduation.

Graduation consists of each trainee receiving congratulations from his trainer and other est staff, along with the gift of a booklet of aphorisms from Werner.

At this point, I think the concept of completing the est training and the graduation can be more accurately depicted if I share with the reader my own experience.

The est training in which I participated ran an exceptionally long number of hours during the entire training. We did not graduate until 4:00 A.M. on Monday. The graduates, who had to be at the hotel by 7:30 P.M. on Sunday, were not allowed into the training room with us until about 1:30 A.M. or 2:00 A.M.

As trainees, we were all told to stand up; that the grads would be coming into the room to share the rest of the experience with us.

Sunday had been a particularly grueling day for me. I was one of the few trainees who felt, even after the trainer had told us that there was nothing to "Get," that I had not "Gotten It." It was my contention that, after everything that happened, I knew "Nothing about nothing."

The friend who had been instrumental in getting me to sign up for the est training had said that he might come down to the graduation. I was incredibly wrung out and exhausted by the ordeal of the training, yet I really hoped I would get to see a familiar face in the graduates who would enter the room.

When the graduates came in, it was one of the nicest and most fulfilling experiences I have ever had. Somehow, I had in my mind that only a dozen or so graduates would ever bother to stay up until all hours of the night to attend an est graduation. They poured through the door, cheering and clapping. Dozens of them came in, until finally there were hundreds of est graduates filling the room! I couldn't believe it. And among those people was my friend. The clapping and cheering must have continued for a good fifteen minutes. I began to rationalize that even if I didn't "Get It," it was worth paying $250 just to be cheered and applauded for such a long time.

Once the grads were allowed into the room, the training continued for another two hours. After that, all the graduates had to leave the room once again and wait outside for the trainees while they went upstairs for their final exercise before graduation. That was the personality profile.

The personality profile is based on a card that has been previously filled out by the trainee, describing an individual they know in terms of the person's name, height, weight, age, build, and marital status. In addition, the card provides three spaces to indicate three adjectives that would describe the person. On the back side of the card are another three lines where the trainee describes three items (nonhuman) and how the person would react to them. For example, the trainee might put down: tennis—he loves it and becomes very enthusiastic and excited when he plays the game. There is one final place on the card where the trainee lists three individuals that the person knows and how he or she should react to those individuals. For example, the trainee might put down that the person would react to his mother in a very negative manner, that he would react to a friend and ask for his friendship and help only when he desperately needed him, etc.

What then happens is that the trainee sits down in a big room on a one-to-one basis with a graduate. The graduate has an unidentified personality profile card with him. He then describes the personality to the trainee in terms of giving the name and the physical description of the personality. After that, he takes the three adjectives and gives the trainee one adjective at a time along with the opposite of that adjective. For example, the graduate might say to the trainee, "Do you imagine this personality to be a happy or a sad person?" Then the trainee would run down how he feels about this personality.

In doing this exercise, many of the trainees are exceptionally accurate in the descriptions that they provide about this unknown personality. est maintains that they are so accurate not by luck, but by the fact that the trainee had the ability to identify this personality from the very onset. The training did nothing more than to uncover this ability. When I completed my personality profile and I did fairly well on it, although I didn't come away feeling that I had uncovered any great aspect of my personality, I raised my hand as I had been directed to do. That was a signal to the trainer that I had completed my personality profile and I was ready to graduate. Then the trainer came over, tapped me on the shoulder and congratulated me. As I walked out of the room, dozens of est staff and volunteers also congratulated me and wished me lots of happiness. I picked up my little book of aphorisms that is a gift from Werner to all of the graduates. It is his way of thanking the graduates for allowing themselves to share in his life.

When I left the est training, I grabbed a cup of coffee and then, exhausted, I headed for home. I was so keyed up when I got back to my apartment that I couldn't go to sleep right away. I did a bunch of things and finally hit the sack. About 8:00 A.M. the phone started ringing. It was all my friends and relatives wanting to find out how the est training had gone for me. When I had finished the previous weekend, I was really high. I felt that est had been one of the most profound experiences that I had ever gone through in my life. And, at the beginning of the second weekend, when the trainer told us that we had only received about fifteen percent of the training, it simply boggled my mind. I felt that if that much had happened to me in one training, the second weekend was going to make a transformed person out of me. And I was really excited about that.

I am in therapy, and I consider that I am winning in therapy. However, I "Got" so much about myself during the est training that I felt it would literally cut years off of my therapy. I recognized things about myself during the est training that I had refused to get close to in any previous therapy.

With all of that input, my friends were expecting miracles. And so when the phone began to ring, and I found that I was more depressed than I ever was in my life, I hardly knew what to do.

I did the easy thing. I brushed everyone off and told them I was exhausted and went back to sleep. When I woke up again some hours later, I was really very frightened. I couldn't remember being as down as I was, and I couldn't understand what had happened to make me that way.

From what I understand today, being depressed as a result of the est training is not an unusual occurrence. Many people feel that way—and I believe I was one of them—as a result of taking away the belief systems that all of us hold onto so dearly. After the belief systems are removed, there is a certain healing process and there is a certain length of time that must elapse while you replace the belief systems with experience. This is not always an easy thing to do, and it wasn't for me. However, the next time I woke up, I tried to look at my depression and to choose it. That helped a little bit. As the day wore on, my depression, for no particular reason that I could identify, began to wear off. By the next day, I was beginning to think I got a lot more value out of the est training from the last weekend than I had originally thought.

One thing that especially came clear to me was the Pain Level Nos. 1 and 3. When I had first heard that lecture, I felt there wasn't much value in what the trainer said. However, in my therapy, I got to work through one situation that had been running my life based on the pain levels that he had described. All in all, for whatever anyone can say about the est training, I felt it really did turn my life around, and $250 was cheap for that experience.

CHAPTER XI

The Post-Graduate Training

Similar to a high school reunion, the Post Graduate Training takes place a few days after the conclusion of the est training. Human nature must be a very predictable thing because the Post-Graduate Trainings are all predictably alike. Grads who never spoke with one another during the training react to one another as if they had been through a blood-ritual initiation together. There is a tremendous amount of camaraderie among everyone in attendance. And, most of all, it is like the end of a religious revival meeting, *after* everyone has cast off their crutches and wheelchairs.

People who knew one another somewhat during the training greeted each other like long-lost friends. Throughout the room, there was a terrific sense of fraternity and brotherhood. Most interesting of all, the majority of the graduates come to the Post-Graduate Training fresh out of their "acts."

That possibly is the most amazing part of the Post-Graduate Training. People are used to reacting in social settings and running their "numbers" on the people with whom they speak. But at the Post-Graduate Training, there is genuine sense of honesty pervading the entire evening.

Conversation with est graduates begins at an entirely different level. If an est graduate asks another how he is, he really means it. It's not done as a socially acceptable kind of thing. And the answer comes from the Truth. As a result of this, strong friendships are often made at the Post-Graduate Training, which continue on for a long period of time. Of course, the est trainings have only been in existence for five years, so the long-term effects of the training cannot be measured. But graduates often comment on the wonderful friendships they have been able to build as a direct result of the training.

Another benefit is that the friendships are different from what the graduates generally have had in the past. Very often, strong friendships had been built on the recognition that the two friends would not call one another on their "acts." Although it provided for temporary emotional stability, that kind of relationship is certainly not the basis for any kind of meaningful, long-term friendship.

New graduates tend to be some of the most enthusiastic people you will ever find. For example, John Denver, after he completed the est training, dedicated one of his albums to est and what it had done for him. Today, John Denver is still a strong supporter of the est movement.

Both of the trainers attend the Post-Graduate Training. Generally, the trainer from the first weekend takes the lead. The first trainer, of course, is the one who took such a strong, commander-type position with the est trainees. During the Post-Graduate Training, the grads get to see their first trainer out of his role. It is often noted by many of the est graduates what a wonderful person their first trainer was. Often, one can find that women grads have fallen in love with their trainers. It is not at all uncommon to hear a female graduate exclaiming over the beauty and body of her trainer, and what she would like to do to him! This is certainly understandable for many women, for the first time in their lives, are being accepted by another human being as perfectly okay the way they are. It allows them to really practice coming from cause and not effect. In safety, they can practice dropping their typically female dating roles and be themselves. For many, this is a new and unusual experience and extremely impressive.

Whereas a woman might fall in love with her trainer, a man often finds the Post-Graduate Training Seminar to be an excellent place to meet eligible women. First of all, they have a fairly good idea of where the woman is at, based on the est training. (For example, they know who the women are that shared their lack of orgasms or frigidity. So now they have a choice as to whether they want to try and conquer these women and "turn them on," or whether to leave them entirely alone in search of a more sexually adjusted woman.) Many women, however, prefer not to go out with any of the men they have met at the est training. Often, they claim to feel much too vulnerable in terms of what they have shared to start dating someone who knows it already. On the other hand, many couples who date as a result of the est training claim their relationships are far better because they start at a level in the relationship much further along than would be normal in the standard dating routine.

It has been said that the beginning of a Post-Graduate Training Seminar appears to be much the same as Maxwell's Plum or any other popular Eastside bar on a Saturday night. Men and women are drifting around, making dates, making friends, sharing experiences, and generally having a good time. It is certainly a lot more like a social setting (except for the absence of "acts") than it is a seminar.

Once the Training Seminar began, everyone was enthusiastic about sharing how he or she had felt since the training ended. Even those people who had not shared at all during the est training were eager to communicate their experiences. A middle-aged man stood up and shared that he had been afraid for the last ten years that he was going to lose his job. Everything he did at work was borne out of fear. After the training, he chose not to work in that kind of existence anymore. He had worked very hard and had done a good job for the company, yet he sensed that the company didn't feel the same way about him. So he went in and spoke with his boss, told him what a good job he had been doing for the company and, as a result, he walked out of the office with a $5000 raise.

A fourteen-year-old boy, who had gone into a catatonic state during the Danger Process, and who had never shared the entire time of the est training, got up and spoke to the entire audience. He said that he had really enjoyed the est training and enjoyed having met so many wonderful people. He was greeted by cheers and applause.

An older man, who had shared earlier in the training that he had never been able to express to his wife just how much he cared about her, shared that in communicating this love to his wife, he had really experienced her for the first time. They had been married for many years, but he felt that the end of the est training would mark the beginning of his marriage.

One man stood up and admitted he was an alcoholic. He felt that he had been using drink as a means of avoiding having to feel anything in his life. He hadn't had a drink since the beginning of the est training, and he felt for the first time in his life that he might be able to lick the problem. He also found, as a result of the training, that facing himself as he was was not nearly as terrifying as he had imagined.

Over the hours of the Seminar, one by one, graduates spoke out enthusiastically about all of the terrific things that had taken place in their lives in the few days since the training had been over. Confrontations with happy endings were related by the dozen. Marriages were improved, children started listening to their parents. Those in therapy got more out of the session or encounter. The room filled with praises.

To think that everyone who attended the est training came away with a perfectly marvelous life change would be an unreasonable conclusion. Indeed, many people came away from the training very depressed and remained that way. Or, they left on a "high" and within a few days, dropped into a real state of depression.

One man, who was the father of four children and whose wife was expected to have their fifth baby the following month, went to his job on Monday morning and was fired. However, he admitted that he really had not been taking on the responsibility at his office that he should have, and he didn't blame his boss for firing him.

One woman shared that, as a result of the training, she went home and asked her husband for a divorce. At the time of her sharing, she wasn't sure whether that was a happy or sad experience for her. The trainer told her to just stay with the experience and to take what she "Got."

Since there is not time in the three-and-one-half-hour session for everyone to share his or her experience, there is a short break given where everyone turns to his or her neighbor and shares what they "Got" as a result of the training. About fifteen percent of the graduates go through the entire est training without ever really sharing. This Process of "meeting your neighbor" and sharing some of what happened during the est training is a good way of practicing the sharing concept and getting over any considerations that an individual might have about it. "Meeting your neighbor" is very similar to a continuation of the sharing Process.

Not everyone leaves the est training and the Post-Graduate Training sure that they really got any value out of the training. The leaders take time out to cover this during the Post-Graduate Training Seminar. As it happens, most people *do* get some value from the est training immediately. Some people get value right away, but they have so many barriers still in existence that they refuse to see the value and it takes a couple of weeks before it finally gets through. And some people can go as long as six months before it finally hits them as to what the training is about and how it works for them. This is simply because the est training is an individual experience. Many times, the trainees resist the training to such an extent that it only remains with them in a very surface kind of manner. Sometimes, not until many months have passed has the resistance diminished enough (because the graduate is aware that it is there) that he begins to get value from the training.

For example, one est graduate whom I interviewed for this book claimed that he had never gotten any value from the est training. He said he had gone through it simply because so many of his friends had and they had seemed to get value from it. Prior to the time of his training, this man had lost a number of jobs due to his cantankerous personality. He was always getting into arguments with people on the job. At the time of the training, he was unemployed, since he had just been fired shortly before he had started est. Shortly after he completed the training, he acquired another job that he has now held for nearly a year. In speaking with him recently, I asked how his relationships were going at the office, and he told me that he felt very good about all of the people there. He said that he recognized his need to be always right and to win arguments and, as a result of that, he tried to be more aware of his pattern and to avoid putting people in that situation. This man, in my opinion, is a classic example of an individual who resists a situation. It is very obvious, after speaking with him, that he got a great deal out of est. Yet, it is too difficult for him to admit that.

At the Post-Graduate Training, there was a lot of pressure to sign up for the Graduate Seminar. Several graduates came and spoke with the people and, during the breaks, there was a concerted effort to get the new graduates to sign up.

However, at the Post-Graduate Training, there is a far different reaction to this than there was at the Guest Seminars. As you might recall, there was a great deal of hostility and anger directed toward the est staff and volunteers who applied such high-pressure techniques to the guests.

This time, there was a much more blasé attitude on the part of the new graduates. They were far more willing to take the responsibility of making the decision in terms of whether or not they wanted to sign up for the Graduate Seminars. If they told a staff member or volunteer that they were not interested, the est person moved onto someone else to speak with him or her about it. At the Guest Seminar, it was rare to find a person who would be definitive about whether or not he actually wanted to take the training.

It seemed, as a result of the est training, that the new graduates did come to choice about the Graduate Seminars and decide yes, they wanted to attend; no, they didn't. As a result, the high-pressure techniques that were applied to them disappeared rather rapidly.

It has originally been stated that the hostility and anger that the guests felt was nothing more than their rebellion against responsibility and making choice. If the reaction at the Post-Graduate Training Seminar was any indication of that philosophy, then it certainly seems to have some merit. If people are willing to take more responsibility in their lives, and they get that as a result of the est training, then it has really done them all some good.

CHAPTER XII

What estians Say

In researching this book, I spent many hours speaking with people who had graduated from the est training. Although feelings of dissatisfaction about est were sometimes expressed, the overall opinion of people with whom I spoke seemed to be that they had really gotten their lives together as a result. (Indeed, most of the criticism is aimed against the Organization of est and not what est has done to people.)

On the following pages, I have described some of the experiences that est graduates have had during, and as a result of, the training. Their real names have been changed.

CONRAD AND ELAINE

Conrad is an advertising executive in his mid-forties. He is friendly and outgoing and loves to be with people. He is aggressive and loves to win, but has a low-key manner. He is good looking and well dressed, with a trim figure.

His wife Elaine is a darling, bubbling woman, who looks much younger than her 46 years. She loves to laugh and has a knack for making people comfortable. She excels at tennis, and although she is competitive, she never puts people ill at ease during a match.

Conrad

I signed up for the training as a direct result of my son having gone to it. He is 26 years old and married to a lovely young woman. I always considered that he was a little on the immature side and had gotten married too early. Although he and his wife seem to be pretty happy, I could sense that there were a lot of problems. He took the est training and I saw dramatic changes. I can't describe exactly what they are, except to say that he and I got along better than we had in years. I have the feeling that Bob was much more at peace with me.

In addition, I am in an industry that is very competitive. I have my own agency, and it requires a lot of effort. I have worked very hard to get where I am today; yet, I didn't always feel at ease in the situations that I encountered on an everyday basis. Although advertising is a service business, I didn't like the fact that I was taking so much crap from my clients. I always felt as if it were their right to lay a lot of "numbers" on me, and I couldn't get myself out of that. After a while, it began to affect me and my business. I started getting tension headaches and drinking too much.

The est training was a terrific experience for me. One of the great things that happened was that my son reviewed the training at the same time that I took it. On the last day of the training, I finally "Got It." I started to laugh hysterically. And when I looked over, I saw that my son, Bob, was crying his eyes out. He was so happy that I had "Gotten It" that he cried for joy. You have no idea how heartwarming that was to me, and how much closer it brought me to him.

I also came to see that my headaches were nothing more than an unwillingness to take responsibility in my business. When I started selling, I would come from a position of experience and professionalism. Today, it's rare that I have a headache, and I have reduced my drinking considerably.

One other thing. It was seven months before I could persuade my wife to take est. It was a nerve-wracking experience while she was going through it, but I believe it brought us ever so much closer.

Elaine

I took the training because after being married for 27 years, I suddenly saw everything that was familiar to me—my husband, my son, my daughter-in-law—start to change. It was a rather frightening experience, and something that I wasn't really prepared to deal with at first.

The three of them would sit around the dining-room table and discuss what they were experiencing and choosing and when they were and weren't responsible. Frankly, I was somewhat jealous and I didn't want to admit it. That was why I had so much trouble getting myself to est. I felt that they all had something that I didn't, and I hated to admit that.

What I "Got" from est was a new sense of life. I recognized that I had been setting myself up so that I could be victimized by my husband and children. That is, I would revolve my life around them. Naturally, there were always changes in what was going on. I would resent that my plans would have to be altered.

Then, I realized that that's where I was stuck. So, I chose it, and when I did, it disappeared.

Today, I feel better about myself than I have ever felt in my life. For the first time, I really feel as if I am starting to live. And believe me, that's a great feeling.

DAISY

Daisy is a young, vivacious career woman, recently separated from her husband.

When my husband and I decided to separate, I really fell into the pits. I couldn't believe that he was going to actually leave me, in spite of the fact that I knew it was the right thing to do.

I suffered a lot of depression and upset. I lost a lot of weight in a short period of time. Although I was very depressed, I knew that I had to do something with my life. I couldn't imagine going through such a painful experience without getting something from it.

In speaking with a good friend, I confided the state of my marriage. He told me to "do est." As much as I am into psychological movements, I had never heard of it. He told me that was a good thing, because then I could really go into it with an open mind. I thought $250 was a lot of money, but he told me that if I didn't feel I had gotten my money's worth from it, he would refund the $250. I didn't think that was such a bad deal, so on blind faith I called est and joined a training.

Well, I have to tell you, it was the most profound experience I have ever had in my life. They weren't kidding when they said that est could turn your life around. It sure did for me.

First of all, as a result of est, I got myself up and out

of the pits. I also threw away my Valiums and sleeping pills. When I can't sleep at night, I just do an est Process, and I drop right off to sleep.

But, most of all, I got over my fear of loneliness. I had never lived alone before, and I couldn't imagine how I would handle it. Well, not only am I living alone and liking it, but I fully recognize that I've chosen it. I know that when I want people around, I can choose to have them around. It's no longer a big thing for me to be alone, because I know deep down that I am really not.

NAT

Nat is a young man in his mid-thirties, with thick horn-rimmed glasses. He is of medium build and height, nice looking, but has a very tense air about him.

I took the est training because I am really nervous about my job and I wanted to get over that. Some of my friends had taken it, and they appeared to have gotten a lot out of it. Besides, they would all sit around and talk and laugh about their experiences in a language that seemed to leave me out a little. I figured I would go and get the training and then I could really be with them and experience what they were experiencing.

Not all that much happened for me as a result of est. I suppose I "Got It," but it sure didn't make any sort of dramatic change in my life. I am still nervous and upset about my job. est didn't help me with that at all.

In a way, I feel like something must be the matter with me. At the Post-Graduate Training, everyone talked about all the great things that had happened to them as a result of est, and I really didn't feel anything.

As a matter of fact, I never really felt anything all the way through the training.

It's a shame, though, because I really wanted to get better. Now I don't know what I'll do; my stomach is always knotted up and I am very tense around women.

I met a really nice woman at the est training. We had dinner together a couple of nights. I thought maybe I could go out with her. But when I approached her at the end of the training, right after graduation, she really gave me the brush-off. I thought she'd been really honest with me, but I felt like a real jerk when I saw her boyfriend waiting for her at 4:00 in the morning.

ANNETTE

Annette is a tall, slender, extremely attractive woman in her mid-thirties. She works for an executive search firm.

At first, I hated est. I had a really bad experience with my trainer. At least, I thought it was bad at the time.

We were all required to fill out a personality profile card. (This is a little card that describes, in detail, someone you know. Not only the physical attributes of the person, but intimate details about his or her life.) I thought that was an unfair thing to do. I couldn't see exposing someone else so completely without the other person's permission. Even though I had been told that the personality profile card wouldn't be read without the trainee's permission, I didn't think it was right for someone else to see it. So, I didn't fill it out.

During the training, I shared that I had not filled out the personality profile card. The trainer was very hard on me. He told me that I had broken an agreement, and that if I didn't fill out the card, I would have to get out of the training.

I explained to him that I was a very private person, and that I didn't think it was right to expose someone else without his or her permission. My private life is very separate from my business life, and I have seen a lot of people get screwed in this business by having things written about them. I was determined that I wasn't going to do that myself.

Anyway, the trainer told me that I was a classic example of the real asshole. He said that I claimed that I was a private person, and yet I had just told 250 people all about myself.

It was very difficult to listen to him throw all that crap at me, and I wanted to throw down the microphone and run out of the room. But I didn't. I stayed. And I was very bitter about him. Fortunately, the next weekend we had a new trainer. So it wasn't so bad.

After the training, I began to realize what an "act" I was running. I claimed to be such a private person because I was really afraid to admit that I needed other people. At the time, it was more important to me to be cool and sophisticated, without ever letting anyone get too close. Now, I understand that this "privacy number" is an excuse to prevent myself from being in touch with what's going on. It's a barrier to experiencing life.

I am a lot more honest and a lot more with it today, and I enjoy life a lot more. It wasn't easy, but I am really glad I went to est.

ALLEN

Allen is a tall, very thin man who looks far older than his 48 years. His thinning, strawberry-blond hair and his poor manner of dress do nothing to add any charisma to his personality. He owns a small printing brokerage company.

I am really glad I went to est. It helped me in a lot of different ways. But I think the most important way it helped me was with my business. I have had it for a number of years and, many times, it has been a real struggle to keep it alive. Some years, I have only taken a few thousand dollars in salary and my wife has had to go out and get a job.

I should have given it up, but I just couldn't stand to fail. I never shared that during est, nor did I even think about it during the Truth Process. But one day, after I had been out of est for quite some time, I just got in touch with the fact that, if I failed, that was okay.

It didn't make a difference anymore. I would make it my responsibility to do everything to create a good solid business. And, if it didn't work out, that was okay. I could always do something else. It was as if an albatross was lifted from my neck. I can't say that my business is doing great, but it has improved. And I feel a lot better about it. Also, I noticed that my wife doesn't pressure me nearly as much as she used to. I think she knows deep down that if it doesn't work out, I will do something else.

LEILA

Leila is a pretty, dark-haired woman, who looks a lot younger than her 33 years. She has a lovely figure that she covers in tight clothes, and she has a certain aura about her that attracts men.

I went to the est training because I hate men and I don't like women so very much, either. Yet, when it comes to a man, I have to have one. Otherwise, I can't stand the loneliness of life.

A whole bunch of my friends had gone to est and told me I should, too. I knew very little about it, but I figured I should join the group.

Anyway, right off, I shared with everyone that I hated men and that I hoped to change that. I really want to love them.

During the Truth Process, I worked hard on my man-hating as an item. I "Got" that I didn't hate men at all. I really hated myself and if a man liked me, that was affirmation of the fact that he was stupid. I then lost respect for the man who cared for me and eventually we would break up.

Now, I am working on liking myself better, and it really helps. When I meet a man, I don't immediately lose respect for him if he likes me. I am in therapy right now, and I feel est helped me a lot in getting me to recognize what I was doing to myself.

JUDY

Judy is a young girl in her early twenties, who describes herself as a "fat-thin person." She is a secretary.

est did wonders for me. Believe it or not, I used to be really fat. My thighs would rub together whenever I walked, and flesh hung over the top of my bra.

One of the things I worked on at est was why I was so fat. God knows, I didn't think I wanted to be that way.

As it turned out, through the training, I got in touch with the fact that I was fat as a way of covering up for *my loneliness. I found it easier to eat than to face myself.*

For the first time in my life, I truly found out what my eating patterns were. I would come home from work at night and stop in the delicatessen on the way to my apartment. There I would load up with all sorts of goodies: macaroni salad, cole slaw, a little chicken salad, a little shrimp salad, some cookies and cupcakes. Then I would snack on these things while I was preparing dinner. By the time I got through all this junk, I didn't feel so badly that the phone hadn't rung once all evening. And, on a full stomach, it was a lot easier to go to sleep.

Then I "Got" what I was doing to myself. I was using food as a means of avoiding responsibility. I was lonely and I was afraid to experience it. I thought it would be really painful and that I couldn't deal with it. But, in the training, I "Got" that it was okay to be alone. And I also "Got" that I felt it was a bad thing to be alone because of what my mother used to tell me.

I was the most unattractive of three sisters. I was always a little on the chubby side. My mother used to tell me that, if I didn't stop eating, I was going to grow up to be an old maid, and that I would have to live alone all my life. No one would ever care about me.

Today, I realize that she did that as a scare tactic in order to get me to lose weight. But for all these years, I have been believing what she said. I made a fat slob out of myself.

Well, I vowed right then and there that I would face whatever I had to and live my life fully. The fear I used to have of being alone is gone and the relationship with my mother is much better.

SUSIE

Susie is an attractive mother of three, in her early forties, who lives with her husband in New Jersey.

My husband took the est training and it did wonders for him. He used to be terribly nervous and upset all the time and after the training, he became much more relaxed. Even his associates at the office noticed it.

He really wanted me to do the est training, and after all he told me (he described the training in detail), I was really curious about going.

He took me to an est Guest Seminar. I must say that it was a good thing that I had already decided to take the est training, because I felt the people at est were terribly aggressive and high pressure. People all around me were getting terribly angry at the treatment they were receiving from volunteers. Sending them on a big guilt trip for not signing up, and all that.

Since I've taken the training, my life has come together in a lot of meaningful ways. I "Get" that I have created a lot of the messes in my life. For the first time, I am willing to take responsibility for them. No longer do I feel obligated to sign up for a lot of charity and volunteer work, which I can't possibly handle, because I want to make sure people think I am nice.

Today, if they like me that's okay, and if they don't like me, that's okay. It's really a nice feeling. A lot of my life has really just cleared up.

MARIA

Maria is a pert, dark-haired woman of Spanish descent. She is a housewife with four children.

I hadn't spoken with my father or two sisters in over four years. I can't even remember why. One day, when we were all together, we got into a big family fight and everyone left in a huff. I was angry and hurt over some trivial thing, and I felt if they really loved me, they would call me.

Well, guess what? They never did. As time went on, I became more bitter and resentful about it. I was miserable, although I would never let anyone know it.

Anyway, after the first weekend of the est training, I spent a lot of time thinking about the Danger Process, where we tried out "being with someone" in the audience. I realized, while I was standing up on that platform, that I really wanted to be with my father and sisters. And I knew right there and then that if I didn't do something, one day my father would die and I would never have completed my relationship with him. I probably wouldn't even go to his funeral.

All that following Monday I thought about what had happened at the est training and how I was being right and keeping my pride at the cost of being alive and experiencing my family. I thought that was ridiculous and didn't make any sense at all. So, I got up my courage and called Daddy.

He was so happy to hear from me, he started to cry. I told him I loved him and that I was sorry for what had happened and that I wanted to see him again. He couldn't say a word, he was crying so hard. Then I called my two sisters—one lives in Connecticut and one lives in California—and I told them both the same thing. They couldn't believe what I was saying. I love my sisters and I love my father and now, at last, we have a good relationship once again. And I'm aware that I chose to knock down the barrier of my pride and experience my relatives.

CHARLOTTE

Charlotte is a very bright, attractive woman in her early thirties. She is open and friendly, and has a real zest for life. She is separated from her husband, and has a full-time career.

During the est training, I got a whole new perspective on my sexuality. I had a bad experience with a man when I was a young girl, and I felt very guilty about it ever since. As a result, I got the idea that life was a lot more favorable toward you if you were a man rather than a woman. I thought a woman's life was comprised of cleaning house and making babies. And I wasn't about to have any of that. I spent a lot of time proving that you can be a woman and still have a good time. Emotionally, I have paid a high price for it.

First of all, I've always felt guilty about good sex, because I thought that was only the man's right. A woman should be much more passive than I. So when I would get into a long-term relationship with a man, I would eventually go from being really turned on by sex to passive to frigid. The less interested I became in sex, the more guilty I became until it was impossible for me to have any sort of sexual relations with positive feelings.

As a result of the training, I got in touch with how really hung up I was in all of this sexuality. I've spent a lot of time working with my therapist and improving the situation. For the first time in my life, I am beginning to experience a little that it's okay to be a woman and to love sex. Without the training, I'm not sure how long it would have taken me to reach that conclusion on my own.

I have someone about whom I really care. When I'm

with him, I really feel good about being a woman. We have the best relationship that I have ever had with a man. And I think it will continue to get better.

MILT

Milt is a small, stooped man in his early sixties. He is the president of a subsidiary of a large insurance company.

The morning I finished with the est training, I was never so depressed in my life. I felt as if my entire world had been taken away from me.

I wandered around the City for a number of hours after the training was over. It was 6:00 in the morning, but I wanted to make sure that my wife would be getting up for work and leaving before I got home. I couldn't bear to talk with anyone.

By the time I got home, she was just leaving for work. I undressed, crawled into bed, and pulled the sheets up around me.

Then the strangest thing happened to me. I began to shake. And then I began to cry. During the entire training, I had never cried or even felt close to it. Now, I just lied there and wept.

This deep, deep depression settled over me. Suddenly, I no longer felt that I even knew what life was about. I felt as if my "act" had been stripped away and I had nothing with which to replace it. I felt more vulnerable than I had ever felt in my life.

I lied there in bed and tried to get in touch with why I was so frightened. I realized it was because I had been living my life all those years without really knowing who I was. And at the end of the training I still didn't know. Except that somewhere during the training, I had shed my "act."

I don't think I have made all that many changes since I went through the est training. I got some of my "act" back, but I threw away a lot of it, too. I am much happier about that.

My business division is doing much better, too. I believe I owe that to the est training. I've been afraid to be aggressive for a lot of my life, and if it hadn't been that I knew some executives high up at the parent company, I don't think I would have the position I have today. Now, when I attend meetings, I'm not afraid to look people in the eye and I am not afraid to say what I think. That surprised a lot of people, and it certainly has helped me.

I think the sixty hours I went through with est were some of the more difficult hours of my life. Even though I am on in years, I still feel there is a lot I can get out of life. And I am going to do just that.

STEVE

Steve is 36 years old, and is in the advertising agency business.

I was in the training room seven minutes when they started to get to me. All of the trainer's remarks seemed to be directed to me personally. You see, I was one of those people who always came from the position that everything was "doing it to me." I believed that my first wife was "doing it to me;" I believed that my girl friend now was "doing it to me;" and my endless succession of jobs was a result of bosses "doing it to me." What est did was to "Get" me clear that it was only me who had been, in fact, screwing up my life. That I had set it up *so that I could lose, because I realized that I got a lot of value from losing.*

At first, the thought that I was totally responsible was very frightening to me. Then, when they told me that I was just a machine and there was nothing I could do about it, I panicked. In fact, the final Sunday night at graduation, all I could think about was that both legs had been kicked out from under me. Everything that I believed in, every place I came from, was, in fact, destroyed. Unlike the other graduates, I didn't leave with a feeling of security or a sense of great joy, but rather I was depressed because now, not only was I clear that I was responsible, but there seemed to be little that I could do about it. As the weeks and days went on, many surprising things happened. It was almost like Werner was on my shoulder saying, "Things will clear up in the process of life itself." While many people seemed to use the training as an opportunity to extricate themselves from relationships they were in, my own relationship seemed to get immediately better. Many people used the training to extricate themselves from jobs they were in, and mine seemed to get immediately better. I started to get along with not only my boss, but my secretary. Clients whom I never seemed to like became nice people, almost as if they were totally transformed. Of course, the only one who was transformed was me.

It all seemed to work. Today, I am interested in going beyond the est training. No, not the Graduate Seminars. I tried them and got very little from them. But, I have become involved in a number of Eastern philosophies. I am now taking Silva Mind Control, which I understand a good deal of the est course was based on, and I am also interested in Mind Dynamics, Scientology, and TM. Maybe because of the nature of the business I am in I somehow get some bad vibes from Werner. But still, I am indebted for the value I got from the training.

KEITH

Keith is 38 years of age and unemployed.

I came to est because my ex-wife said that I needed it. At first, my immediate reaction was that it was another one of her crackpot ideas. But the more I seemed to read about it and hear about it, the more I thought it might have some value. I went to the Guest Seminar and was definitely turned off. I had very negative feelings about the person running the Seminar and about the whole concept, but to be perfectly honest, there were all of these very attractive young ladies there and I thought the worst that could happen was, by the end of the four days, I would come up with some incredible phone numbers.

I must admit that I was tuned out of the first six hours of the training. I was busy having mental sexual experiences with all of the foxy young ladies who were in the room. And then, suddenly, although I wasn't there, all of a sudden I was there. It was like everything he said was starting to fall into place. All of a sudden, I "Got" the part that that was the way I had led my whole life. I wasn't really interested in anything that anybody else was saying. All too often, my penis instead of my mind was running me. The more I tuned in to the training, the more frightening it all became. Several times during the course of the training, I thought of getting up and running out. As a matter of fact, at one point, I gently slinked toward the back of the room. I was immediately confronted by the training supervisor who wanted to know where I was going. And I explained that I had had enough of it. In my heart, I knew I really wanted to be talked down and back into my seat. But, there was another part of me that was saying, "This is all too painful." The training supervisor ended the debate when he said, "Yeah, sure, yeah, sure, you can leave, like you've been doing everything else in your life, running away from it. Why don't you just stay here and look at yourself for a change?" I slinked back to my seat.

The 55 hours in that room seemed like 355 hours, and I can honestly say I went through more emotions in those four days than I have gone through the whole rest of my life combined.

Even now I am not sure what the training all means, or what it is all about, or if it works. I can only say that it put me in touch with a lot of the kinds of things that I had questioned all of my life. Most of all, it put me in touch with myself—someone I had worked very hard at not getting in touch with.

JACKIE

Jackie is 32 years old. She is employed as a department store buyer.

Unbelievable . . . the whole experience is unbelievable. I have spent most of my adult life in therapy. At age eighteen, I started college, because it was the thing to do. Later, I continued to go because it became a crutch for me. My therapist was very supportive of the way that I lived, and support was something I never got at home, at work or anyplace else.

People talk about the price of bread going up, or the price of sugar or milk. I guess I judge inflation in view of therapy. I started out paying $15 an hour to a *therapist. Now, some years later, I am paying $50 an hour. It's funny, when I heard about est, my main consideration was the money consideration. Blow $250? Then I realized I had probably spent somewhat over $20,000 on psychologists, psychotherapists and marriage counselors. In fact, this very year, I was programmed to spend $2000 in therapy. So, what was another $250? I am now perfectly in touch with what my problem is, and although I don't wish to share it for this interview, I can tell you that my problem is something that I was just starting to get at after all of these years of therapy. And, on the first day of the training, during one of the Processes, it all came to me. It all came crystal clear as if someone had handed me my problem neatly carved up on a plate.*

CHAPTER XIII

Questions and Answers About est

The purpose of this chapter is to clarify any questions that the reader might have about est. It is not designed to represent the official est philosophy; it is rather the judgment of the author based upon his personal experience of the training and discussions about est with graduates, staff members and media people.

Q. What is the purpose of the est training?
A. According to est, the purpose of the est training is "to transform your ability to experience living so that the situations you have been trying to change or have been putting up with clear up just in the process of life itself."

The graduates, however, feel that the purpose of the est training is simply, "to make their lives work." Others believe the purpose of the est training is to make them happier, and still others consider it an easier way to deal with the problems they are currently facing.

Many people state that the purpose of the est training is to make you better. Werner Erhard says, "The purpose of the est training is not to make you better. I happen to think you are perfect exactly the way you are. . . . The problem is that people get stuck acting the way they were instead of the way they are."

Q. If est says that you are perfect the way you are, why do you need the training?

A. So you can get in touch with the way you really are. Most people are so busy doing their "act" that they have lost sight of exactly who they are.

Q. If est says that you are perfect the way you are, do they mean that Adolf Hitler was perfect the way he was?

A. Yes and No. They mean: yes, Adolf Hitler the person was perfect the way he was. However, he was busy doing his "act." And as the history books so clearly state, his "act" was hardly perfect. The man behind the "act" was, in fact, perfect. We, the people behind our "acts," are all, in fact, perfect. The problem is simply that we develop a belief system or operating philosophy that moves us away from our real selves.

Q. What does it mean to be "perfect the way we are"?

A. The est philosophy states that there are three you's. These three you's are:

1. The "you" that is put out before the public. This is the "you" that is covered by an "act." It is the social self.
2. There is the "you" that is deep-down inside. It is the one of which most people are afraid. It is the bad "you," the antisocial self.
3. There is the real "you." This is the "you" that is perfect in every way and is the one to get in touch with.

Q. Is est therapy?

A. The est Organization makes a strong point of maintaining that it is not therapeutic in any way, nor is it therapy. However, many graduates refer to the process as therapeutic. Some claim they were able to get in touch with facts that ten or more years' of therapy were just starting to uncover. Many graduates report dropping out of therapy upon completing the est training since they no longer needed therapy or got value from it.

Q. Does est, therefore, not approve of therapy?

A. The official est policy is that you should be doing whatever you get value from that doesn't hurt anyone. If you get value from therapy, then you should continue with your therapist. However, one of the basic premises of the est training is that you are responsible for everything in your life and that you have created it all. If you are going to a therapist for "help," simultaneous acceptance of the est philosophy therefore means that it will be difficult for you, in good conscience, to continue your therapy. If, on the other hand, you are going to therapy for "assistance," then, for sure, you will want to continue the process of therapy. (See the glossary for a discussion of the difference between "help" and "assist.") Many therapists feel that there are people who are not stable enough to go through the est training. Others may disapprove of it simply because they are losing many of their clients to it. Others lack enthusiasm even though they have seen remarkable improvements among their patients. The feeling among the psychological community varies widely. It's important to note that est specifically will not permit someone who is in therapy to attend the training without permission of his or her therapist. And the Organization also advises you not to attend the training unless you are "winning in therapy."

Q. Is est like therapy or like an encounter group?
A. Yes and No. The training has some of the aspects of therapy in that a good deal of sharing takes place and some people with psychological training refer to this as having a cathartic effect. On the other hand, the form is actually quite different. The training has none of the combat encounter kind of feelings experienced in a Synanon encounter group, for example. Nor does it have any of the "touching" that is usually associated with Esalen-type encounter.

Q. How does est feel about religion?
A. If religion works for you, then you should continue with it. Some of the aspects of est, however, are really counter to organized religious training. This is because in the est training *you* are God, meaning that you are solely responsible for your life and its actions. Therefore, you cannot look to any supreme being for special treatment, goodness, or award. One graduate laughingly said that the reason he turned away from religion after the est training was that his "religion was concerned with life after death, and [he] was suddenly interested in life after birth." In fairness, it should also be reported that other graduates have experienced deep religious feelings at the conclusion of the training. It's important to conclude with the statement that est will not interfere with religion, so that you will not be threatened during the course of the training with any of your religious beliefs. It is worth noting that est offers a special scholarship plan for mem-

bers of the clergy in an attempt to expose these important members of the community to the value of the training.

Q. Is est brainwashing?

A. No, by definition. First, the Webster definition of brainwashing includes that a person must be held against his or her will. Obviously, everyone at the training is there voluntarily and stays voluntarily. Further, the purpose of brainwashing is to change your belief system. est maintains that the purpose of the training is not to change a belief system, but rather to put you "in touch" with the way you really are. Some graduates refer to the est experience as implanting the "est way of life;" as educating the individual to be responsible for his or her actions, for creating everything in his or her world, and for being a machine, therefore, unable to change. To the extent that implanting a belief system is brainwashing, then one might say it is brainwashing.

Q. What does it mean to say that "being right is costing you your life"?

A. One of the three "you's" whom we mentioned earlier was the first one, the "you" who puts on an "act." As part of this "act," it is essential to be right. Most of the time, being right is more important than the sense of being alive and experiencing ourselves the way we are. Frequently, being right involves making the other person wrong. For example: after a hard day at the office, a husband becomes incredibly angry with his wife over a minor issue. She points out that they had previously agreed on this issue. He denies it, even though he knows she is speaking the truth. It's been a brutal day. He can't bear the thought of apologizing . . . just yet. He argues until he "wins." They sleep in separate bedrooms that night. Being right is costing him his life—his aliveness.

Q. How do I register for the est training?
A. The following is a list of est offices in which the training is made available:

ASPEN
Post Office Box 3221
Aspen, Colorado 81611
(303) 925-8050

BERKELEY/OAKLAND
3101 Telegraph Avenue
Berkeley, California 94705
(415) 548-6400

BOSTON
46 Beacon Street
Boston, Massachusetts 02108
(617) 227-0460

CHICAGO
1825 North Lincoln Plaza, Suite 214
Chicago, Illinois 60614
(312) 337-6100

DENVER
231 Milwaukee Street, Suite 206
Denver, Colorado 80206
(303) 320-6557

HONOLULU
1200 College Walk
Honolulu, Hawaii 96817
(808) 521-5644

LOS ANGELES
1102 Broadway
Santa Monica, California 90401
(213) 393-9635

NEW YORK
300 East 40th Street
New York, New York 10016
(212) 682-6700

SAN DIEGO
2180 Garnet Avenue
San Diego, California 92109
(714) 270-7880

SAN FRANCISCO
1750 Union Street
San Francisco, California 94123
(415) 441-0100

SAN JOSE
828 McKendrie Street
San Jose, California 95126
(408) 247-0775

WASHINGTON, D.C.
3240 Prospect Street, N.W.
Washington, D.C. 20007
(202) 337-8080

Q. How much does the est training cost?
A. Two hundred and fifty dollars. Paid in advance.

Q. This seems like a lot of money to me for four days
   in a hotel room. Why does it cost so much?
A. est says that the Organization shows a minor profit
   from the training and that all of the money is re-
   invested in the Organization to build it, expand it,
   and serve the graduates. They state that:

1. The cost of constantly expanding the Organization and opening of new offices is significant.
2. The cost of communicating with graduates and prospective trainees is significant. They refer to the fact that their postage and telephone bills are astronomical.
3. Much free work is done in the community. est has run a training, at no cost, at Lompoc Prison and has also done workshops in Watts at no charge.

However, many view this as a weak explanation for a multimillion-dollar superstructure. Specifically, at this writing, some 80,000 people have gone through the training, and there are an estimated 100,000 who will complete it by the end of 1976. Simple arithmetic puts that at a gross business volume well over $20 million. Since most of the members of the Organization is volunteers, many graduates find it hard to imagine what happens to all the money.

Q. Is est a non-profit organization?
A. No. est is incorporated as a profit-making institution. All of the stock is owned by a trust, but est is not willing to disclose ownership. Some critics point out that if est's big cost is postage, they should apply for non-profit status. Then, they would be able to mail at the non-profit rate of 1.8¢ per letter instead of the current postage rate of 13¢. Why don't they? Most critics feel this is due to their reluctance to open their books and explain the distribution of their funds. The est Organization says that, for numerous reasons, they are incorporated as a profit-making institution.

Q. Is Werner Erhard getting rich from est?

A. Werner's official salary is listed as $48,000 a year. Some critics point to the Mercedes-Benz that he drives and his large house in Marin County as lovely fringes. However, est's Public Information Office says that the Mercedes was a gift from relatives, and the house was not bought using est funds.

Q. If the training really works, why are people concerned about Werner's income?

A. Some people are concerned and some aren't. Concern stems mostly from the honesty policy, rather than what happens to the money. That is, as one graduate said, "The sixty hours was the most valuable sixty hours of my life. My feeling is that I have my racket and Werner has his. It's just that his is working better. If he is making millions of dollars, God bless him, he deserves it." Some graduates say that it's okay for Werner to be making this money, but that he should simply admit to it. One of the basic tenets of the est philosophy is that your life doesn't work unless you are honest. Critics find it hard to believe that such an efficient organization, with all those thousands of volunteers, is not able to show a profit on a gross of over $20 million. It is interesting to note that, by and large, graduates are not concerned with the money aspect simply because they feel that they got value for their $250. One graduate whom we interviewed for this book said, "I have paid my therapist over $8000 in the past couple of years and got very little for my money. I paid est $250 and got aliveness. I think it's the best money buy I ever made."

Q. Can a couple go to the training together?

A. Yes. However, they will *not* be permitted to sit

together during the training. Many couples report tremendous value from having experienced the est training together. They were able to communicate about their experiences. However, others report that they were hampered in their sharing because they were afraid of the value judgments that their spouse or partner might make.

Q. Is there a lot of emotional stress involved with the training?

A. Yes. It can be a very frightening experience to reach past your social self and get in touch with the real you. Until one experiences that "it's okay not to be okay," the training can be both frightening and emotionally unsettling. Also, the very nature of the sharing processes and data, as well as the physical environment, provide a stress situation for many trainees. It is not at all unusual during the course of the training for people to cry, vomit, faint, and even laugh hysterically when there is nothing particularly funny happening in the room.

Q. Why don't they let you go to the bathroom?

A. Because it works. Every part of the training is designed for this one purpose, and one purpose only. In the experience of est and Werner, the maximum value can be obtained only through the specific rigors that are set up for the trainees. Others refer to the fact that not going to the bathroom, not eating, and emotional tension in the room is designed to "push all your buttons." By making you uncomfortable, the trainer is able to more quickly press through your natural defenses in order to get in touch with the real you.

Q. A friend of mine told me that the basic tenets of the training are "follow the instructions, take what you get, and keep your sole in the room." What does this mean?

A. Some of the instructions may seem vague, at times, although they are always specific. The trainee is simply asked to follow the instructions as he understands them. For in this method, what's needed to "come up for him" is exactly what will happen. The reference to "sole" in the room is not a metaphysical reference to the "soul," but literally refers to the sole of your foot. The purpose they have in mind is that only by physically being there can you " 'Get' the training."

Q. What are the actual hours of the training?

A. The training runs from 9:00 A.M. each day until the work of the day is accomplished. Usually, this is around midnight or 1:00 A.M. Sometimes, trainings end as early as 11:00 P.M. Sometimes, trainings go until after 4:00 A.M.

Q. Don't people get sleepy and hungry?

A. Yes. Many people get to experience hunger for the first time. And within that experience, according to est, they get value. The experience of sleepiness is interesting, too. Usually, the room is kept quite chilly, which will often keep the trainees from falling asleep. However, some graduates report sleeping through as much as two-thirds of the training and still getting value from the experience.

Q. Does Werner Erhard currently do any trainings himself?

A. No.

Q. A friend of mine had an excellent trainer. Is there any way I can register for this man's particular training?

A. No. est feels that the trainers are identical. The purpose of the trainer is to "get out of the way and give you the space to be you." The data is identical at every training. Therefore, it would not matter who the trainer is. In addition, est certainly does not want to start a policy of favorite trainers. The official opinion is that you will "Get It" whoever the trainer is and wherever the training is held.

Q. How should I dress for the training?

A. Be comfortable is the basic tenet of the training. Sitting on a hard chair for some twelve to sixteen hours is a difficult experience in anything but the most comfortable clothes. In addition, it is advised to bring a sweater or a jacket. The room frequently becomes quite chilly.

Q. I hear that they use a lot of dirty language and four-letter words. Is this true? I find it offensive.

A. Yes. So-called foul language is ever present in the training. According to the trainers, the words themselves don't have any inherent meaning. (Clams casino and shit are the same.) Therefore, it is only the value you place upon them. If you are offended by foul language, one of the things you will want to get in touch with during the course of the training is why you find it offensive. As a trainer said in one group, "All words are the same. The meaning and the value and the offense that you place upon them all exist only in your own mind."

Q. Can you leave during the training without losing your money?

A. Yes and No. There are three distinct times during the training in which the trainees are given the option of leaving and receiving a full $250 refund. However, if one chooses to leave at a time other than these specific opportunities, they must leave and lose the entire $250.

Q. Why must I wear a name tag?
A. Because it works. est finds that wearing a name tag adds to the value of the training. Some trainees hypothesize that this is helpful in developing a camaraderie among those experiencing the two-weekend training. Others feel it is simply a help for the trainer to identify people by name. One other prevalent theory is that wearing a name tag, in fact, puts you in touch with your own identity.

Q. Does the training wear off?
A. Not usually. Most graduates indicate that they continue to receive value from the training as time goes on. In fact, some state that the value improves over the months rather than decreases. The purpose of the training is not that you come away with any specific information, but rather that it gets you in touch with yourself and the way that you deal with the world. This can probably be explained more simply as the difference between wisdom and knowledge. That is, wisdom is a general ability to understand, whereas knowledge is specific transmittable information.

This theory has, obviously, not been tested over a long period of time since the training, as we know it, is less than five years old. In addition, the majority of graduates, on a purely statistical basis, have been through est in the last twenty-four months. Therefore, the long-term effect is hard to judge. Unquestionably, some graduates report coming out of the training "flying" and weakening as time goes on. Some of this is prevented by the Graduate Seminars that are offered. Others take advantage of the special opportunity to "review" the training for $35 any time after graduation. (Six months must elapse from graduation date before a "review" of est is permitted.)

Q. Must I take the seminars that are available after graduation to receive the full value from the training?

A. No. The training is total by itself. Many graduates feel that they want to avail themselves of the Graduate Seminars to keep in touch with the est principles and to enhance the value of the training.

Q. Should you date est graduates?

A. Yes, if it will work for you. Many people report that they have had meaningful relationships with people with whom they have shared the training. Often, they are able to start the relationship on a much higher plane. That is, none of the usual cat-and-mouse type of dating games. They have already shared all types of things about themselves and both have experienced a great deal about themselves in the training. Therefore, they are both coming to the relationship with a higher knowledge point.

Of course, one needs to add that there is nothing self-selecting about the est process. That is, virtually everyone is accepted for admission who fills out an application form and pays the cost. (Also, if you are seeing a therapist, you must get permission from the therapist to take the training.) One of the many trainees whom we interviewed for this book said, "One of the reasons I wanted to take the training was that I had heard you could meet a lot of foxy ladies willing to go to bed." Specifically then, people who are basically unethical do not come out magically cured from the four-day experience.

Q. How do I become a volunteer?

A. Upon graduation, you call the est office and advise them that you would like to serve. There is an important part of the training in which it is outlined that "serving one who serves" is a very high space. Graduates are encouraged to volunteer for a specific period of time (minimum of three months). Many volunteers report receiving tremendous value from serving, even if that serving is so menial as addressing envelopes and filling out name-tag cards. Other volunteers have come away with the feeling that they were being "used" by the Organization and feel resentment that there are millions of dollars coming into the est Organization while they are providing services free.

Q. How do I become a trainer?

A. Many people who complete the training want to become trainers. What is actually set up is a long and difficult process. Becoming a trainer requires total dedication. Randy McNamara (a trainer), for example, reports that his first assignment was to prepare Werner's tea. Randy only became a trainer after he was able to get in touch with the fact that it really didn't matter whether he was preparing tea or doing the training. One trainer shares that his first jobs were so menial as cleaning the toilets. In many ways, becoming a trainer is almost set up as in the old Zen system of how one becomes a *roshi*. To become a *roshi* (guru) requires long years of dedication and there is almost a self-selecting process in terms of those who survive the rigors.

Q. What does it mean when they "push your buttons"?

A. Having your "buttons pushed" is the predictability that you will react in a certain manner. For example, if the trainer tells you that you are an ass-hole and you constantly respond with anger and a denial of that fact, then the trainer is "pushing your buttons" and you are always responding in a constant manner.

When your "buttons are pushed," the est trainer will often refer to the fact that you are acting like a machine, *i.e.*, giving the predictable response. This is something to recognize and be aware of since it is a very important part of your pre-estian life.

Q. Can a child attend the est training?

A. Yes. A child can attend the est training but he must be more than fourteen years of age, and the parent with whom he lives more than six months of the year must be an est graduate.

Q. Are there other special trainings available for children who cannot meet this requirement?

A. Yes. There are several special training sessions designed entirely to meet the needs of children. The child can be of any age under eighteen, and his parents do not need to have attended an est training, although this is very helpful. Generally speaking, the amount of time that is devoted to the est training for children is less than that spent for adults. This is because the children "Get It" sooner than the adults. It is believed that children have less of an ingrained belief system and fewer barriers to overcome in order to obtain the value of the est training.

Q. Can I attend the est training if I have a medical problem?

A. Yes. There are special provisions for people with medical problems, whether it be a necessity to eat at a specific time, take medicine at a specific hour, exercise, or rest.

All trainees with a medical problem must bring a note from their doctor stating what this medical problem is. All trainees who have special medical requirements must sit in the last row of chairs so that they can be properly served without disturbing the other trainees.

Since there are no timepieces allowed in the room, the people with medical problems cannot be aware of the time. Therefore, they let the volunteers and staff know beforehand what time they must receive their special attention and they are notified by an est volunteer when it is time for them to take their medication.

Q. Are there any age limitations for taking est training?

A. No. You can be as young as six (to take the children's training) or any age on the other side of the scale. For example, in my training there was one 75-year-old grandfather who was there because his grandchild had asked him to share the experience. I understand that the oldest est graduate is 96 years of age.

Q. If est believes that someone has created everything in the world, does that mean "I created babies being napalmed in Vietnam?"

A. Yes. This is probably a difficult concept to look at as an isolated incident. However, true estians believe they are responsible for such far-removed events as plane crashes, wars, and ultimately whatever one person does to another person. Stewart Emery, who was est's first trainer and former chief executive officer, has said, "Although people are told not to believe anything the trainer says, under the circumstances in which the training is delivered they will go away believing some of the stuff that they absolutely shouldn't believe."

Q. Isn't all this fury about creating everything a potentially dangerous psychological concept for many people to handle?

A. Possibly. There is the story about a father who wanted to commit suicide after the est training because he believed that he was responsible for his own son's suicide. On the other hand, most people leave the training feeling that all they need do is take the responsibility factor only as far as it should logically be taken. That is, they have previously blamed their failures on their husbands, wives, the government, their bosses, and other people who are not, in fact, responsible. Yet, when it comes to points that are obviously outside of their control they are willing to accept the possibility of coincidence. For purposes of the training, it is probably most effective that the trainer take the point of view that nothing is an exception; and once he should break down on any point of that argument, the entire focal point of the training would no longer work.

Q. I understand that many people on the est staff absolutely worship Werner. Isn't this also a potentially dangerous situation?

A. Perhaps. Although Werner does not require devotion to him personally, he does require total devotion to duty. est staff members report that they have no rights or privileges when they are working for Werner. The purpose is only to serve the Organization. This, of course, helps to get the job done. The danger comes in possibly as one volunteer stated: "Sometimes I have the feeling it was all like *The Manchurian Candidate*, that Werner was going to call us all up to vote for him."

Q. Isn't est really just another version of Silva Mind Control?

A. No. Although certain processes have striking similarities to Silva Mind Control processes, many of the techniques are quite different. There are also techniques within the training that bear a similarity to Scientology, Gestalt, Zen and Mind Control. The sum, however, is more than just the total of the parts. The effect of putting together all of these disciplines and adding some original material creates a totally new package which is, in fact, est.

Q. What kind of changes does one see in people who have completed the est training?

A. The results are frequently startling and remarkable. The changes include financial, spiritual, physical, emotional, and psychological. People report their income doubling almost overnight. Others report failing marriages beginning to work. Slouchers stand up straight. Depressives become manics. And the company wallflower becomes outgoing and popular.

Q. Does everyone "Get It"?

A. Almost. Not everyone likes it, but most everyone "Gets It." Knowing that you are totally responsible for everything in your life can be a very frightening and nonsatisfying experience to many people, and some ignore it.

Q. Everything I read about est makes it all sound so good. Isn't there anything bad about it?

A. Possibly. Some people report an initial depression after the experience. Others report that it was simply like a weekend in the Bahamas, somewhat relaxing but wore off after a short time. Still others have characterized est as a rip-off. However, by and large, most people have left the experience feeling it was the most valuable time they have ever spent in their lives. Most of the criticisms of est have little to do with the training. It is rather criticism leveled at Werner Erhard, the army of unpaid volunteers, or the hard-sell technique involved in building up the Organization. As one graduate put it, "The four days were terrific; it turned around my life; I feel so alive. As far as Werner and the Organization, I think he has got a fast-talking, money-making deal going and those guys who work for him for free are meatballs. . . . However, that doesn't make the training any less than what it was—wonderful."

Q. I understand that Werner Erhard and est have attempted to get an injunction against the publisher of a book that is not favorable toward est. Is this true and, if so, doesn't this poorly reflect the Organization's theory that communications are the essence of life?

A. Yes. est did proceed with an injunction against Carl

Frederick's recently published book, *Playing the Game of Life*. However, the case was thrown out of court. Communications *are* the essence of life. est brought the injunction against Frederick's publishing company because Werner felt that the author was using est concepts and materials to promote himself while est had invested a tremendous amount of money into building its reputation. The book is out now, and so are many others.

Q. I understand *Psychology Today* magazine recently had an exposé of est. Is that true?

A. Yes and no. The exposé was really one person's (Mark Brewer's) experience of the training. The est Organization has prepared a statement refuting several dozen inaccuracies within the article.

Q. Do I have to speak in front of the group and share my experiences?

A. No. Although at several times during the course of the training one is urged to share, there is no requirement to actually get up and speak. In addition, one can obtain true value without actually talking before the group. For example, the author of this book never spoke during the four days, and still found the training to be worthwhile. The purpose of the sharing is obtained even if you individually are not one of the sharers.

Q. People seem to have a lot of trouble explaining the training and why it has been of value to them personally, as well as how it works. Why are people so reluctant to share the techniques?

A. Because it is difficult to explain them. One reason is that, although the trainee may receive the benefit of the training, he does not necessarily understand, on an intellectual basis, why it has worked. est says it is because the training is an individual "experience" and, as such, cannot be explained. For example, the experience of eating steak is totally different than telling someone about what it is like to eat steak. One graduate told the author, "It was like me trying to explain to my roommate what it was like when I had my first orgasm."

Q. I am pregnant. If I attend est training, will my baby get the value of the training?

A. No, according to most psychologists. Yes, according to est. Most psychologists have told us that experiences of mothers are seldom transmitted to babies. Early psychological literature is filled with stories of pregnant mothers who attended museums so their babies would be interested in the arts. Modern science has told us that this is simply not true. est, however, tells us that pregnant mothers will transmit the training to their babies by the very fact that the mother is sitting in the room.

Q. I've heard that some people get very depressed as a result of the training. Is that true?

A. Yes, it is true. The est training is not an easy thing to go through. During the course of sixty hours, trainees are generally in touch with every emotion possible. Additionally, they cover many painful experiences from their past.

It is not easy to go through something like this, but for the most part, the trainees get value from it.

It is not uncommon to be depressed as a result of the training. Very often, this results from the trainee being in touch with his "act." After a lifetime of living in a belief system, it can be very frightening and depressing to find that you have been living your life in a non-experiential sort of way. Often, the trainee will feel vulnerable. He has given up his "act," and hasn't yet replaced it with anything. Given time, the trainee will get in touch with the fact that being depressed is okay. Once he recognizes that, the depression will generally disappear. Also, with a little process, the trainee begins to learn to replace his "act" with honesty and responsibility for himself. When he does that, he is on the road to living a rich, full, and alive life.

Q. Is it true that Werner demands absolute worship from his staff?

A. Yes and no. Werner demands that all his staff and volunteers take complete responsibility for their lives. He also demands that they take complete responsibility for everything that goes on at their jobs. And it seems that they do. Recently, a special rule was enacted at est that states that staff and volunteers can't work past 9:30 at night. This was done because so many people were working because they wanted to until the wee hours of the morning; they weren't getting to have any other sort of life. Werner's staff and volunteers are all very dedicated people. They dedicate themselves to est and to its leader, Werner Erhard.

However, I have spoken with a number of volunteers and a few staff members who are no longer with est. These people all say that Werner *does* demand absolute devotion from his staff. And, if he doesn't get that devotion, he will ask the individual to leave the Organization. It is important to keep in mind that most est staff receive very little money for their jobs. Volunteers, of course, receive nothing at all. Therefore, the kind of person who is working for est is doing it not for the money, but for the love. This often leads to a certain kind of "worship" about the company and its founder.

Q. What is the beach that I hear everyone talking about?

A. This is an imaginary place, and it is directly involved with doing the processes. The processes are a meditative exercise where the individual can go and get in touch with a variety of situations. For example, a process can be used to relax, or go to sleep, or to get rid of a headache or sickness, or to work out an item that is troubling the individual.

The beach is a place that an individual has created in his imagination. The beach is to be a favorite place the person likes to go to, or it can be a beach made up in the imagination that combines all of the best assets of sand, sea, sky, etc. from a person's travels around the world.

During a process where an individual wants to relax, he would go to the beach at the end of the process as a final relaxing place. The beach is always safe and the individual does not have to put his "act" there. If an individual were using a process to work out an item, he would go to the beach after he had worked out the item. Going through an item (troublesome situation) can be an exhausting experience. The beach enables the individual to relax and put himself back together again after the ordeal.

Q. What is the center?

A. The center also involves the processes. It is a place that the trainee or est graduate has within him, which he has built (in his imagination) within himself.

Generally, it is a room or little house that contains everything the individual would need to live and be happy. Anything the individual especially likes or wants to have can be brought into this center.

The most important part of the center is that it has a special door that allows the individual to bring people in and out. The purpose of this door is to allow a means of getting people from the outside world into the center.

In a way, this is a very therapeutic process. If an individual is troubled by another person, he can (in his imagination) bring that person into his center for a discussion. In this way, he can talk with the other person and work out what is bothering him and what he feels about the situation and the other person. Very often, this will end the problem right then and there. However, sometimes it only makes it partially disappear. And sometimes, as a result, the individual will have a real talk with that person based on his discussions in the center. By working it out first in his own mind, it gives the individual an opportunity to see what his reactions will be and to experience them.

Q. What happens during the training that causes people to throw up?
A. Nothing. It's a very individual experience. Sometimes, people throw up when you would think there was absolutely no provocation for it. They throw up because something is going on within them as a result of the training.

Everyone's life is different, with different experiences and different ways of experiencing. The training might very well recreate an extremely painful past situation for an individual. This might not be the case for anyone else. But what is going on in the training may bring out such painful memories that the person actually vomits as a result of them.

In addition, very often during the training, people are afraid. Fear is another very big factor in causing an individual to vomit.

The great majority of people do not throw up during the training. Perhaps a half dozen do in all. Throwing up is sensational. Therefore, it tends to get a lot more coverage than the ordinary things that happen. If you have ever read any articles on est, you notice that the media does not make a lot of references to the happiness, laughter and wonderful times that are shared. It is always much more dramatic to depict vomiting, crying, screaming, etc.

Q. What is the est chart of thought?

A. This is a chart, devised by Werner, which divides up the mind into two basic mental functions: Experience and Non-Experience.

It is Werner's theory that most people spend their entire lives in a non-experiential state. This means that they are constantly acting out a belief, reason, understanding, logic, etc. According to Werner, these basic tenets are the worst way by which to live your life. Non-experiencing leads to being ripped-off and victimized.

Only when you are coming from cause can you really experience life. It means throwing away all of the beliefs, concepts and logic that you have heretofore known and understood.

The purpose of the chart is to give the trainees some sort of visual sign of what they have been going through, so they know where to reach. Only when a person experiences living will he be able to transform his life.

Q. Why do people go unconscious?

A. People go unconscious because they do not or cannot face themselves and the idea that they have been putting on an "act" all their lives. When people think they may have to part with their social selves (and give up their "act"), they become very frightened. As a result, they will find all sorts of conscious and unconscious excuses to avoid the situation. People become drowsy; they fall asleep; they leave the room; they get hives and allergies; they get sick; they fall down and break a leg—the excuses go on forever.

Only when a person truly experiences life can he or she face it. At that point, he or she will not go unconscious anymore. This is not to say that a person will *never* go unconscious again. However, when it does happen, people are generally much more aware of what they are doing. As a result, they will often stop and examine what they are doing and what their motivations are.

Q. I have heard the training room referred to as a "safe room" or a "safe place." What does that mean?

A. During the training, the trainee is free to share anything that comes up for him. He will be sharing this information with 250 other trainees and the trainer.

By assuring the trainee that the room is a "safe room" or "safe place," it means that he can say or do anything he wants to (within the confines of the law) and nothing he says or does will be used against him, at any time, for any reason.

This concept of creating a "safe place" is expanded into the trainee's everyday life. For example, the center that he has created within himself is a "safe place." If he communicates with another est graduate, it will probably be "safe" for him to do so, since the other person will also understand and accept the same ground rules for not using any information or data that is provided to him.

Creating a "safe place" for yourself is a very important thing to do. It enables you to acknowledge what is going on with yourself and others. This may be in the form of a grave confession, a secret, an inspiration, or whatever. But the very important thing to remember is that the place represents safety. The person with whom you share this information must let it mean just that.

Q. If one partner in a relationship takes the training, and the other one doesn't, will it hurt the relationship?

A. Yes and no. The training can be a beautiful and meaningful experience for the individual who goes through it. Most often, trainees come out of the training, at some point, very excited and "high." Lots of things have happened for them during the training that they had not previously recognized or experienced. It is their natural inclination to share it with someone whom they love.

Since the training is very much an individual experience, it is often quite difficult to communicate it to another person. Therefore, if the trainee wants to share the experience with his partner, he may not be able to clearly describe it. This can be very frustrating.

Sometimes, the individual who did not go to the training feels very threatened by it and, as a result, does not wish to discuss it at all. Then, est becomes a real sore point between the partners. The one who is so excited about the experience is no longer able to communicate it to the person whom he most wishes to do so. This can be a real problem, and is often a vital sign that there is a problem in the relationship itself.

However, as a result of the training, people very often become much more alive, positive about themselves, and happier. This has to reflect in their relationships with other people. As a result, the other partner will benefit from the experience.

Q. Isn't est a lot like Gestalt Therapy?

A. est and Gestalt Therapy are similar in one respect. Their original thesis is based in the principles of personal responsibility. est maintains that you can only begin to experience life when you take responsibility for your life. Gestalt Therapy is very similar in its conclusions.

However, that's where the similarity ends. Werner has taken the best of Gestalt Therapy, *i.e.*, personal responsibility. In addition, he has used many other disciplines in his training. Mind Dynamics, a company for which he worked for a number of years, figures dramatically in est. So does Psychosynthesis, Taoism, Zen, Psychocybernetics, the Bible, Scientology, etc.

The big difference, of course, is that with all of the disciplines, you study to understand or believe them. With est, you take the training to experience it. You might say that est has its beginnings in the endings of every other discipline.

Another thing to remember is that each discipline doesn't have an exclusive on its concept. That means there is a lot of overlap between all of the disciplines. For example, Yoga and Zen overlap. Dale Carnegie and the Bible overlap. Mind Dynamics and Mortality Consciousness overlap.

Instead of trying to figure out exactly where est

comes from, it is much better to accept it the way it is. Either it works for you or it doesn't.

Q. I have heard a lot of negativity about the Guest Seminars. Could you tell me a little bit more about them?

A. There are two kinds of Guest Seminars. One is a seminar that is devoted entirely to non-est grads and/or trainees. This is usually a very large seminar, and the majority of people are there to find out more about est. The second kind of seminar is one in which guests are allowed to attend, but they cannot sit through the entire thing. For example, guests can attend the Post-Graduate Training Seminar, but they are only allowed to be there for a small portion of it. Then, they are taken to another room where they have their own mini-Seminar.

It is very true that a lot of negative comments have been made about the Guest Seminars. The comment most often heard is the one that refers to the aggressive, hard sell people get to sign up for the est training. A good deal of the people who have been to Guest Seminars are very resentful of the treatment that they received from est staff and volunteers.

However, the est Organization maintains that they are only bringing people to choice about the est training. They claim that people are so resentful because they are rebelling against taking responsibility for themselves and making a choice.

In spite of all this negativism about the Guest Seminars, the plain facts are that in spite of the aggressive behavior of the est staff and volunteers, plenty of people are signing up at the Seminars for the training. That's kind of funny when you think about it. All these people are yelling and screaming about how awful est is and how aggressive the staff and volunteers are, yet they are going ahead and taking the training and loving it!

Q. Is there a lot of pressure to sell your friends after you have completed the est training?

A. There is a lot of pressure if you allow yourself to be stuck in it. Many people say that est staff and volunteers infer you will not get the full value of your training if you do not get friends and relatives to share the experience with you.

The est training is comprised of whatever you get from it. This means that if you don't wish to bring any friends to Guest Seminars or other lectures where they are invited, you don't have to, and you don't have to feel obligated to. Feeling pressured into having to bring friends and relatives is often an indication of insecurity on your part. For example, by bringing a friend to a Guest Seminar, you might feel that you will be better liked by the est staff and volunteers. That is completely irrelevant. The most important thing is that you have to like yourself. That's your responsibility.

Often, as a result of the training, you will want to bring friends or relatives to the Seminars in hopes that they will sign up for the est training. That's perfectly okay. It is nice to be able to have friends and relatives with whom you can discuss the training, the experiences, and what it means to you. It is much more difficult to do this with people who have not experienced the training. A lot of times it is impossible to discuss it with other people, because they simply do not and cannot understand what you are talking about.

Q. I have heard that there is a terrific process where you eat strawberries and lick stones. What is that?

A. On the second Saturday, after the trainees return from dinner, they find little cellophane bags under their seats. The bags contain one large strawberry, one daisy, one slice of lemon, one stone, one square of wood, and one square of metal. This bag of "goodies" is used in the process which follows.

The purpose of the process, though it may seem trite, is to really experience a strawberry, a daisy, a slice of lemon, a stone, a block of wood, and a block of metal. Most people have never really looked at and experienced any of these items.

For example, when you bend back a lemon peel, geisers of oil shoot up from it, like flames from the sun. Also, by pulling off the green leaves, you can look deep down into a strawberry. Metal can have a very distinctive smell and wood has a definite texture. The purpose of the process is to observe all of this and to experience it.

It is an extremely happy process. Lots of laughter and joy are expressed while people examine the items that they have been given. It is one of the few times during the training when the trainees can talk without being reprimanded (although it is not officially sanctioned to talk during this process).

This process takes place after the dinner break. There is a general concensus among the trainees that it is a good thing that this process is not conducted before dinner. Otherwise, everyone would have gobbled down his or her single strawberry and lemon section without ever having had a chance to experience it.

Generally speaking, if you talk to an est graduate, he or she will remember this process with particular fondness. It is a lovely, relaxing break from all the emotional pressures in the training.

There is one other particularly important aspect to this process. It is an excellent way of demonstrating that life doesn't always have to be terribly serious. You can also get a lot out of life when you are having a good time! est graduates have really had a chance to experience strawberries and daisies and lemon sections. As a result, they are more likely to have the desire to experience other things that they would normally take for granted. This is a very important angle on life.

Q. How come Werner is so sure that everyone is going to "Get" the est training?

A. The est training is an individual experience and, therefore, everyone will come away with something different. Even if a person says he "Got" nothing, that is something. People may not like what they "Get" and therefore choose to ignore it, but what they "Get" is certainly laid out before them.

Much of the training is very simple and common sense.

The purpose of est is to transform your ability to experience living. If you slept through *all* of the est training—almost an impossibility—then you experience that you didn't want to face what est was about. That's something.

The main tenet of est is that you have to take responsibility for your life. Your problems can't be due to someone else's actions. This is repeated over and over and over again during the training.

Also, everything that goes on in the training goes on because it works. People are not allowed to smoke, eat, be aware of the time, stand up, talk, go to the bathroom, etc., because it allows them to leave the room. The longer they are in the room, the more aware they must become of themselves and the situation that they are in. The training processes nurture all of that.

Additionally, there is another major factor that helps most everybody to "Get It." Almost everyone who takes the training is there because he or she really wants to be there. The individual may have conjured up all sorts of excuses as part of the "act" but, basically, no one is keeping that person in the room except that person.

Q. If the basic tenet of est is for each of us to take responsibility for ourself, why doesn't Werner take responsibility for Jack Rosenberg?

A. Werner claims that he has taken responsibility for Jack Rosenberg (the name by which he was christened in 1935). He also claims that he has taken complete responsibility for the wife and four children he deserted a number of years back. Indeed, they have all been through the est training.

Although Werner originally changed his name after he left his first wife in order to cover up his identity, if anybody asks him about his past, he will release information about it. He experiences that as taking responsibility for the situation. He supports his first wife and four children, as well as his second wife and three children. However, he likes his new name and identity and he plans to retain it.

Q. Why is there so much negative material written about est, and does it really deserve all that heat?

A. Whenever people deal in the unexplainable, there is bound to be a great deal of heated turmoil surrounding it. est is a perfect example.

est is comprised of aspects of nearly all of the

Eastern disciplines and many of those from the West. Believers of one discipline or another are always claiming that est is derived solely from their discipline. This is not true.

Much of what goes on is not understandable or clearly communicable to non-est graduates. Even est graduates don't clearly understand what happens to them during the course of the training. And neither do many of the staff and volunteers. They "Get" what they "Get" as a result of experience, not understanding. And that is basically what est is all about.

When it happens that people can't clearly understand a new theory or philosophy or attitude, they often become fearful or skeptical of it. They hear graduates talk about the miraculous things that happened to them during the training. And in today's day and age, with technology being where it is, there are no more miracles.

When people have different ideas and opinions, and especially when they are significant, they are often ridiculed and treated unfairly. Everyone knows what happened to Joan of Arc. Today, no one will burn Werner Erhard at the stake but, instead, there will be many times when he is unfairly criticized and given a lot of unnecessary heat. That is the cost of living.

One interesting note that is applicable here is Werner Erhard's theory that everything that happens to you, you create. According to that theory, all of the criticism and all of the ridicule and all of the misinterpretations and the lies that have been printed about Werner Erhard were created by himself!

Q. Is it true that celebrities who attend the est training get special attention?

A. est denies that celebrities get any special attention whatsoever. On the other hand, it would not be inconceivable to imagine that they do receive VIP services.

Celebrities have the potential to do a great deal of good for the est Organization. Remember, est does not spend five cents on advertising for any of their seminars or trainings. Everything is done by word of mouth. That means graduates are telling their friends and relatives about their experiences and hoping or persuading them to attend other seminars.

If a celebrity such as John Denver is on a television special that is being broadcast nationally and he raves about est, it's very likely to do est a lot of good. John Denver has thousands of fans who are very malleable and could easily be persuaded to attend the training, just through a single reference from him. In addition, John has written a song to est as a result of the terrific things that happened to him in the training.

Q. I have heard that the celebrities have someone special to work with them when they do the personality profile at graduation. Do you think that is true?

A. More than one est volunteer has stated that the celebrities, upon graduation, have a person with special training work with them on the personality profile. However, no active staff member has ever confirmed this.

One of the purposes of the personality profile is to allow graduates to get in touch with the fact that— according to what they have learned in est—everything that has ever happened in the world and everyone who has ever existed now exist as a record or image in a person's mind. Therefore, if the celebrity is particularly accurate in going through the personality profile process, this concept is more likely to be reinforced as an experience. And if the experience is good, then the celebrity will leave the est training with positive feelings. This means that est is liable to derive a great deal of publicity from all of it. Whether or not there is a special person assigned to a celebrity in order to insure quality in the personality profile process is unconfirmed, but it certainly makes sense.

Q. What is a personality profile?

A. During the est training, all of the trainees are given a small, white card that they must fill out. On this card, the trainee is asked to describe an individual whom he or she knows. Specific information is requested, such as the person's name, age, height, build, and marital status. In addition, specific adjectives are called for to describe the individual; for example, optimistic, sad, etc. The card also asks the trainee to provide information about three inanimate objects and the personality's expected reaction to them. For example, "His dog. Loves him. Is very gentle and sweet with him." The last part of the card requests the trainee to name three people who are known to the individual, what each of their relationship is to that individual, and how he or she reacts to these people.

Then, during a process, as each trainee closes his eyes and goes into his space (semi-meditative state), a graduate or some other person sitting across from the trainee reviews the personality profile card and gives some of the information to him. For example, the trainee is told of the personality's name, height, age, build, marital status, etc. When it comes to specific adjectives describing the personality though, the trainee is told what the adjectives are and is also given the opposite adjective. For example, the graduate would say to the trainee, "Do you imagine this person to be happy or sad, optimistic or pessimistic, self-centered or outgoing?" Then it is the trainee's responsibility to describe what he feels about the personality. Naturally, the graduate has the personality profile card in front of him at all times and is able to refer to it.

It has often been said by trainees and graduates that, during the personality profile process, the graduate or est staff member consciously or subconsciously leads the trainee in the description. For example, if the trainee said that he felt the personality was outgoing, the graduate or est staff member might respond by saying, "Right, right, very good;" and when the trainee gets on the wrong track, he would get no or little response from his questioner.

It would not be so inconceivable to imagine that a celebrity could be "helped" along in this manner, and given indications that could lead to a surprisingly accurate personality profile. If a person comes away from the experience feeling as if he really knew an unknown individual, it could be a very dramatic and mind-blowing kind of experience.

Q. Do you have to practice the processes each day after the est training is completed in order to get the full value from est?

A. No. Many times, the est graduates never do another process. But many of them make these processes part of their daily lives or at least use them on a consistent basis.

For example, one of the processes learned in the est training is a most effective way of putting oneself to sleep at night. If an individual is unable to fall asleep, he can do one of the processes to assist him, thereby avoiding the necessity for a sleeping pill.

Another process that est graduates use is one where the individual can wake up in the morning without an alarm clock and feel refreshed and good, even after just a few hours' sleep.

Sometimes, a graduate will have a particular problem or situation with which he is having difficulty dealing. Then he can use the process that can bring an outside person into his center and work out the problem or situation with that person.

There are many ways to use the processes in your daily life, but that does not mean that an est graduate ever has to use any of them at all. The processes are a function of the est training. Werner finds them to be useful in assisting people to clear up situations that they have not been able to clear up previously. For many people, doing the training is enough. Others like to carry the processes over into their everyday lives where they benefit a great deal from them.

(Author's Note: Since I took the est training, I have never again had a problem with sleeping. I used to take sleeping pills at least three or four nights a week. Now when I have difficulty falling asleep—and I still do—I just do the process that relaxes me and sends me off to sleep.)

Q. Why does est feel it necessary to have the trainees recreate unpleasant life situations?

A. By this you are probably referring to the Truth Process. And, indeed, during this process the trainees often recreate unpleasant life situations. However, they do it by choice. They are not forced to work through anything that they do not specifically choose to work through.

It is very important to remember a basic philosophy of the est training here. One of the reasons why most people's lives are not working is because they have never really experienced living. All of their situations prior to the est training have been in the form of non-experience experiencing; *i.e.*, a life dominated by beliefs, understandings, logic, and reasonableness. That is why people are hung up in the unpleasant life situations that have not cleared up for them. It is simply a matter of them never having experienced the situations.

As a result, during the Truth Process while the trainees are under the direction of the trainer, they are guided through a process whereby they can actually recreate the situation that they have been trying to clear up. *There is one important difference this time—they will experience the situation.* As a result of experiencing it, the situation will often clear up by itself.

The second most common thing that happens is that the experience no longer becomes as important in the person's life. That means that the person is left dominated by the unpleasant life situation, and can either continue to recreate it to clear it up or to choose it as a way of clearing it up.

Q. I understand that everyone has to get up and say "hello" at the Pre-Training Seminar. What's that all about?

A. It's about saying "hello." But it also has another purpose. By saying "hello" to everyone at the seminar, the trainees begin to experience, to a small degree, a process known as the Danger Process.

Toward the end of the Pre-Training Seminar, everyone is required to get up, walk around the room, shake hands with all the people who are there, and say "hello." They are not to say "hi," "how are you?" or any other greeting. The instructions are to simply shake hands, look the other individual directly in the eye, and say "hello."

Surprisingly, this is a very difficult task for most people. The tendency of the trainees is to cast their eyes to the floor and mumble "hello," mumble "hi," or mumble "how are you?" It's also a dramatic depiction of the fact that most people don't carry out instructions—and they don't carry out instructions because they don't want to take the responsibility for them.

If a person is instructed to shake hands with a person, look that person directly in the eye, and say "hello," and he doesn't do that, then he has broken an agreement by not taking responsibility for the instructions. And that's just the beginning of how people's lives get mucked up.

Q. What is the Danger Process?

A. The Danger Process is a sophisticated form of saying "hello"! On the first Sunday of the training, after the dinner break, the trainees come back to a room that is filled with several long rows of chairs. The trainees are instructed that the first row of people will walk to the front of the room where there is a platform. They will stand up on the platform, behind an indicated line, and look out into the audience and make eye contact. They are not required to do anything except to stand up straight, keep their hands at their sides, refrain from talking, and make eye contact with other trainees.

This is a very difficult thing for a majority of the trainees to accomplish. They start to laugh, cry, scream, go catatonic, vomit, etc. This is one of the more dramatic processes, and it is often written up in newspaper and magazine articles. And truly, it is an experience to watch all of these trainees with their varied and frightening reactions to just standing and looking at other people.

It is a startling realization of how well refined people's social "acts" are. They are so busy putting out the "self" that they feel everyone wants to see and know, that when it comes down to just plain being with someone—stripped of their "act"—they can't handle it.

The Danger Process is often a real turning point for est trainees. For the first time, they get in touch with how much varnish they have put on themselves as a protective coating. As a result, there are often major changes in the personalities of est trainees, even during the first week. The Danger Process is an effective working method in the est training.

Q. What happens if you break a big agreement during the training, like getting stoned or drunk? Do you have to start all over again?

A. At the beginning of the training, during the Pre-Training Seminar, all of the ground rules are laid out to the trainees. They are told that they are not to smoke, take drugs, take medicine, or work with other disciplines during the course of the training. They are requested to do this because Werner has found that it works.

However, it is explicitly detailed to the trainees that they do not have to follow any of these ground rules. They make the agreements to adhere to the ground rules by choice.

If an individual gets drunk or takes dope during the training, he doesn't have to start all over again. He should recognize though that he has broken an agreement with est, and that is something that keeps his life from working.

In addition, if an individual is under the influence of alcohol or drugs, it can be a real deterrent in terms of that individual facing himself. In other words, if his senses are dulled during the training, he is very likely to miss out on "Getting It." The human body will do anything to help the mind avoid facing life's situations. Drinking and taking dope are perfect examples.

If the trainee is really interested in experiencing life and getting the most value out of the training, he will refrain from doing those things that will interfere with his getting the full benefit from the training.

If the individual does break a major agreement such as those described above, it is important for him to recognize what he has done and to take the responsibility for it. This is often done through sharing during the training. Interestingly enough, at least fifty to seventy percent of the trainees break one or more of the agreements during the nine days of the training.

Q. Is it true that all of the trainers are required to model themselves after Werner?

A. Needless to say, est has denied this fact. However, you can't ignore the fact that a good number of the trainers look, act, and dress almost identically to Werner.

It is often said by people who have taken the training that the trainers do all look like Werner and dress in the same manner; i.e., the snug-fitting slacks, the open-necked sports shirt, and the well-fitting pullover sweater. In addition, nobody at est is fat! Apparently, they have all gotten their lives together enough that they don't feel the need to have food as a source of fulfillment; rather to supply their bodies with essential nutritional requirements.

However, one can't overlook the fact that all of these people are very dedicated trainers who work at est for low salaries (usually far below what they could have made on the open market in their true professions). They are all coming from a position of Werner's true value to the est Organization. Since they are such dedicated men to the est cause, and since Werner is representative of est, it would not be an unlikely consideration if, indeed, they all did model themselves after him.

Q. I understand that most of the female trainees "fall in love" with their trainer. Is this true?

A. Very often, there is a lot of infatuation on the part of the female trainee. It is not unlike a situation where a doctor has saved a patient's life. There is much gratitude on the part of the patient, and often as a by-product, the patient thinks she is in love with her doctor.

The same kind of idea holds true for the est training. Everyone goes through a tremendous emotional upheaval. During that upheaval, the belief systems of the trainees are very often cast aside and replaced with much more positive feelings of self. Naturally, if another individual is instrumental in assisting you to be that way, it would not be unlikely that you would feel extremely positive toward that other person. That's the kind of thing that's easy to get mixed up with love. In addition, most of the trainers are young, nice looking, and well built. Combine that with the fact that most people will do anything to avoid looking at *themselves*. That includes going to sleep in the training, trying to find an excuse to get out of the room, and fantasizing about being in bed with your trainer. That can occupy a lot of hours and smooth over a lot of emotionally tough situations during the training. If the female trainee does "fall in love" with her trainer, she should try and be aware of what she is really doing during that time.

CHAPTER XIV

Is est Worth All the Aggravation?

When you have finished reading this book, you may feel that the est training is simply a bunch of garbage. That would not be an unreasonable point of view, since much of the est training, even with the carefully constructed explanation, seems to make little sense. And to say that the reader has to experience est is certainly an unsatisfactory answer.

So the question still remains: "Is est worth all the aggravation?" And "Is Werner Erhard a fraud, bilking money by the millions from pathetic individuals seeking 'enlightenment'?"

The answer to the above will have to come, for the time being, from the personal experience of the dozens of graduates with whom I've spoken, as well as from myself. Unfortunately, the est Organization has not been around long enough for any detailed psychological studies to be completed as well as analyzed for the overall implications of est and for its long-term effects on people who take the training.

Almost without exception, est graduates whom I interviewed got real value from the training. I spoke with two executives who headed up good-sized companies. One of them, an est convert, absolutely insists that everyone who works with him take the training. Now granted, "forcing" employees into the training is not exactly allowing them to take responsibility for themselves, but the point is that this man was willing to put a lot of money behind all of these people to get them through the training.

The other executive has been much subtler in his approach. He *suggested* that his people take the training. The choice is up to them. If they choose to do est, and they are not happy with it, he will refund their money. However, he told me that if one of his key executives didn't take more responsibility as a result of the training, he would fire him. (If he's fired, that person will have quite a "soap opera" to spill at the Post-Graduate or other Seminars.)

In spite of the fact that almost everyone I spoke to got great value from est training—whether or not they were willing to admit it—the greatest concern shared by all of the graduates was the background of Werner. And his background is colorful. For a man who was a meat packer, a construction worker, and a door-to-door salesman, it is difficult to imagine that a few years later, without any formal schooling and little formal training (Mind Dynamics), he is capable of emotionally revolutionizing segments of a society.

I think this is why there are so many questions as to what Werner is getting out of the deal. After all, he claims to get very little . . . $48,000 a year. The fact is that Werner owns a profit-making corporation, and he has every right to make as much money as he can, within the confines of the law.

I think a lot of the hostility, distrust and uneasiness about Werner goes back to the notion that every human needs to be right. Basically, it's part of survival. Everyone, at one time or another, has suffered a serious threat to his ego when he chances upon a person who is smarter, more efficient, or more successful than he. At least once in a lifetime, the situation will be so acute as to create a Pain Level No. 1 experience. After that, the human mind is operating on a Pain Level No. 3 basis—the need to survive.

est on the one hand represents a real opportunity for average, middle-class people to transform their lives. As a result, they clear up life situations, just in the process of living. Through est, the individuals experience responsibility and choice. As a result of the training, there are often dramatic life-style changes. It's hard to deny the value of the training if you wind up with a good relationship with your father for the first time in twenty years, or you stop arguing with your wife, or you become more successful at the office, or if you feel a lot better about yourself. When your migraine headache disappears, and your asthma clears up, you can't deny that something valuable is happening.

On the other hand, as a result of a Pain Level No. 1 experience, chances are good that most individuals are operating out of a need to survive. They need to avoid the risk of learning from someone who is smarter than they. They are reacting from past situations, instead of what is happening in the present. As a result, they are coming from effect, rather than cause, when they discuss the est training.

Time after time, graduates stated that they were resentful of Werner's salary, or his car, or the devotion and following that he has acquired. This thought was brought up so many times that I, who had never questioned it, began to think about it seriously. Was est really worth all that aggravation? And was Werner bilking money by the millions from pathetic individuals seeking "enlightenment"?

Certainly, the est training is not an easy thing to experience. Speaking from my own personal experience, I felt it was one of the most difficult self-encounters I had ever been through. Without question, it was the most difficult in terms of the number of hours spent against it. Yet, the overall results of the est training were a transformed me. My parents had divorced when I was young and that, combined with other factors, led to a lessening sense of self-worth. One thing that I "Got" perfectly clear about in the training was that it was a guilt number that I had laid on myself for many, many years. As a result, when I finished the training, I took positive steps in my therapy to correct that situation. (I was always aware that it existed, but I had never clearly experienced it the way I did in the training.) Today, although I have been through a major crisis that ordinarily would have set me back a good way, I feel really good about myself. And I'm perfectly clear that I'm going to stay that way.

In spite of the fact that I experienced more pain and anger and sorrow and grief in sixty hours than I can remember in my life, it was really worth it. There is so much emotion floating through you during the training that you hardly notice the aggravation.

As far as the search for enlightenment is concerned, we all know what is happening with the pop-psychology movement in the United States. The search for enlightenment is a direct result of the wants that society is so busily creating. When a human being is totally occupied with clothing and feeding and sheltering himself and his family, he has little time to consider his personal happiness. Once he moves past the purely need-motivated stage, the human being has time to think about just that. There is more leisure time than ever before. As a consequence, hundreds of thousands of people are questioning their aliveness. Peggy Lee so neatly summed it up in her song that she made famous: "Is That All There Is?" People are constantly questioning it: "Is there more?" It's reflected in the fact that 80,000 people will have completed the est training by mid-1976. And the movement is only five years old!

So what does it all mean? Is it really worth $250 to "Get It"? This book attempts to answer the question "What is est?" est intends to answer the question "What am I?" How successful est is will be judged a decade from now. No one today can really say if it's just another California fad or really the secret of life. And regardless, that's okay.